Be Your Pathfinder

A Guide to Accelerating Your Success in Life, Career & Business

Victoria Okuku

For information about reproducing parts from this book, write to pathfindersmasters@gmail.com

Copyright © Victoria Okuku, 2020. The content in this book is a compilation of the work of the author. The published work is subject to the copyright of the author and any attempt to share in part or otherwise any aspect of this book without the expressed permission of the author is an infringement of copyright laws. All rights reserved.

ISBN: 978-1-7772333-0-3 (pbk)
ISBN: 978-1-7772333-1-0 (ebook)

Be Your Pathfinder

This book is dedicated to God almighty, the sole originator and creator of all paths. Without him, there would be no pathfinders.

To the one holding this book, my reader of inestimable value: you are the reason I am a pathfinder, and I hope reading this book will set the stage for you to become a pathfinder, too.

Contents

Thank you 9

Introduction 11

Chapter 1.   Explore 15

Chapter 2.   Revealing You 27

Chapter 3.   Transformational Growth 41

Chapter 4.   The Game-Changer 53

Chapter 5.   The Power of a Coach 63

Chapter 6.   Test the Waters 73

Chapter 7.   Expect the Unexpected 85

Chapter 8.   Just Breathe 97

Chapter 9.   Five R's to Success 111

Chapter 10.   Tragedy of Isolation 121

Chapter 11.   Seasons 131

Chapter 12.   Cycle of Life 141

Chapter 13.   Carve the Path 149

Chapter 14.   Perform to Rule 159

Chapter 15.   Your Voice & Your Story 173

Other Book from the Author 183

Thank you

Chris Okuku, just inscribing your name brings tears of joy to my eyes and unforgettable memories. You are a great support system, my soul mate for life, my hero, and the wind beneath my wings. It was you who looked at my first few lines of writing and told me the blunt but honest truth: "If you must write, you have to empty all for the world to feast on." You made me understand that writing a book is no mean feat. I am a great writer and a better woman because of you.

To my famous four, my children: David, Sharon, Daniel, and Derick, I can only imagine the sleepless nights you went through for my sake. I remember those nights you stayed awake and listened as I read aloud what I had written and how you gave me your input. You were my very first editors and reviewers, despite your tender ages. You sold out your time for me to become who I am today. I love you beyond description.

Mom and Dad, Mr. and Mrs. P. Bassey: You taught me tenacity and made me understand that hard work pays off. Your value of living right has been my guide and still is. To my other mom, Mrs. Lucy Okuku: From you, I learned how to stay committed to true love and how to love without boundaries.

My siblings: Felicitas (IB), Louis, Henry, George, Big Ben, and Brian, you are truly the best. To my amiable in-laws: Frank, Emmanuel, Matilda, Hilda, and Helen, you are an unbeatable team.

Treasure Ochojila, you are a shining example of a true friend. Thank you for your unflinching support through this process. Because of your die-hard commitment to friendship, I am stuck with you.

To Ehi Ade Mabo: You came into my life at the right time and season. You propelled me to take the step of faith towards actualizing my dream. You are a real game-changer and a fellow pathfinder. I salute your tenacity in what you do, "The mindset surgeon."

And finally, to Grace: You are indeed a representation of what a book coach should be. You looked at my manuscript and reeled with laughter. I will never forget that experience and moment when I had to go back to the drawing board to reorganize my manuscript. Your timeline set my tail on fire, and in less than four weeks, I was able to deliver a masterpiece of a manuscript. It was not easy, but it was worth it. I can never thank you enough, but all the same; thank you.

Introduction

In a world of over 7.7 billion people, most people are continually searching for the blueprint on how to carve a successful path in their personal lives, businesses, or careers. This leaves them with a struggle of identifying who they are, what they want to become, and how to make it happen. If this sounds like you, then you have found the right book, the right compass, to provide direction on navigating through your journey to success.

Like most people, a time came when I was desperate for success. In my quest, I spent hours reading and listening to great people that I may or may never meet in my lifetime to guide me through the process. Along the way, I earned a Bachelor of Science in Microbiology from Nigeria and a Diploma in Early Childhood from Toronto, Canada. I also earned Certificates in Health and Safety and Human Resources from the University of Calgary, in addition to the numerous courses I acquired.

In an attempt to discover my purpose, I lived and worked in different countries. I volunteered for various organizations in diverse capacities and hopped from one job to the other. These were implemented with the hope that it would satisfy my inner desire for carving a successful path. But sadly, the more I hopped, the more insatiable and confused I became.

At last, it dawned on me that inner fulfilment is attainable when we work in line with our purpose and God's will. With this understanding, I decided to let go of those jobs in pursuit of my unique goal. Making the decision was the beginning of my journey to self-discovery.

Over the years, I have taken numerous risks and tread new territories, to ultimately become a pathfinder. Some of these were bumpy and rocky, while others were smooth and easy. Many times, I have broken down in defeat and also celebrated victories. I call those seasons my "bittersweet moments." Along the way, I made several mistakes; some of which were costly but afforded me the experience of a lifetime. But in all, I'm grateful to God for the opportunities and experiences. They serve as a roadmap to my rising.

I have chosen to share my winning strategies on how I turned those trials into triumphs to become a pathfinder. I believe it will inspire someone to take a step in the right direction. Experiences shared can add beauty to one or two lives. Through my experiences, I have birthed different coaching programs to help people explore new paths in their education, business, and careers.

This program came at a time when most people struggled with broken focus and dreams. These people are easily attracted to wanting to do a lot of things at the same time. They seem to fall for anything that crosses their path and appeals to their heart. It makes them lose sight of who they are and what they want to become. This act, if not curtailed, may cause them to spin in circles and tossed in every direction.

You are not only destined to walk in people's paths but to carve a path for yourself and for others to step in. True pathfinders do not only pave a way for themselves, but they also take the lead for others to follow. This book will give you the in-depth knowledge needed to turn your struggles into big wins. Thank you for picking up and reading this book. Be Your Pathfinder is the perfect book with a capacity to maintain and keep you on a successful track.

CHAPTER 1

Explore

> Not all those who wander are lost —J.R.R. Tolkien

One of the most painful experiences in life is to see people who are destined for greatness settle for less because they are too afraid to explore. We are born to be curious from birth. The need to explore is an integral part of our existence, and even newborns are no exception to the rule.

I remember visiting a friend with a nineteen-month baby. The child stole the moment due to his constant crawling all over the room; this made us struggle to maintain a reasonable conversation. No amount of persistent interception from the mother could stop him from daring to explore his environment. He was left alone after a few minutes to carry on. His die-hard attitude got me fascinated as I took a keen interest in observing his actions. He crawled to nearly all the nooks and crannies, picking and dropping items until he touched a very warm object. He quickly dropped it, paused for a moment, and then proceeded to another spot.

Some of the items he picked were quite exciting to him, while some were not. I could see him smell, bite, gaze, squeeze, and rattle some of those items while listening to the sound. Children are great at exploring. They are curious about their surroundings and engage their five senses of touch, smell, hear, taste, and sight when undergoing this process. They go all out while exploring. Irrespective of the number of times they face resistance, these children are unstoppable. It is in exploring that they are able to discover the world around them. Their identity and personality are framed based on their experiences and inquisitive nature as they grow older.

The world is an adventure where exploring is critical to discovering who you are and actualizing your maximum potential. How will you unveil your authentic self and what you can do if you don't explore? Those who are too afraid to step out may become strangers to themselves. A great singer or writer will never know how incredible he is, if he fails to search deeper. To explore is to live. Augustine of Hippo rightly said, "The world is like a book and those who do not travel read only one page."

As we grow older, our curiosity begins to dwindle, making it difficult to reach the pinnacle of our lives. This hinders us from digging deep to unravel who we are. It is crucial to go out and chase after your dreams; you have nothing to lose. Permit yourself to see the world through the lens of a child; be curious to unlock those hidden potentials that are safely and carefully tucked away in your heart. Until you explore to discover your authentic self, you will continually live in denial of your capabilities. Great explorers are great at discovering, and so explore to unveil your unique self.

Discovery

> *The greatest obstacle to discovery is not ignorance. It is the illusion of knowledge* — Daniel J. Boorstin

The mistake of a lifetime is a lack of identity. It is a tragedy not to know who you are, what you want, and what you can do. It is like having a name, yet not able to identify it amid other names. If this resonates with you, don't worry, you are not alone. There are quite a handful of people who are caught up in this web too. In the quest for success, some people are confronted with the issue of lost identity. They tend to emulate those they have high regards for, which makes them to dress, talk, walk, or live a lifestyle that does not reflect their true self.

Those who act this way are clueless about the reason for their existence. Later in life, distraction may set in and causes them to lose touch of those attributes that defined them. They forget what they loved doing as children and allow friends, parents, teachers, society, and those they respect to steer their will in different directions. This lifestyle makes them evolve into who they are not, but who others want them to become. One of the ways to overcome this is for them to stay in tune with their inner being.

Wake up call

Setting your priorities right is a step in the right direction towards self-discovery. You don't want to start a building without a solid foundation, because you may wake up one day to realize that everything you laboured for has collapsed. It is your sole responsibility to take ownership of your life.

Some people embark on numerous tasks at the same time, which could jeopardize efficiency. Multitasking is a great skill to have especially when you have a lot to accomplish within a short time. Being attentive to the tasks at hand can mitigate mixed priorities. There are certain activities that should not go together; like answering a call while driving or watching television while studying. In order to yield maximum results, one engagement must supersede the other. Prioritizing enlightens you to know which activities need urgent attention and which one can be revisited later.

At some point in my life, I struggled with handling multiple tasks simultaneously, without completing any. It affected me so much that I was always behind schedule. The reality of my actions dawned on me when I had to stay up late against my wishes to complete overdue tasks. Catching up with pending tasks was quite overwhelming. This nagging habit gave me a hard knock. My physical, emotional, and mental well-being were affected. Based on my poor productivity level, it was evident that I lacked a clear insight into the importance of prioritizing.

The quality of my work was not satisfactory because they were executed in bits and pieces. Most times, I fell below average rather than excelled. With the event that unfolded, I knew the moment had come to set my priorities right. This marked a turning point and the beginning of my journey to self-discovery. There are strategies for self-discovery; it does not happen by accident. You often hear words like, "You don't climb a tree from the top." Setting your priorities right begins with knowing and understanding what you can comfortably handle per time.

Limiting beliefs

As a new immigrant, I acted on most of the things I heard and perceived to be true, for fear of rejection. I was informed that my last name, "Okuku," would hinder me from getting a job because it is indigenous, and I believed it. For the most part, I accepted being called Victoria Chris, instead of Victoria Okuku to gain acceptance. As a person of colour and accent, I was also told that venturing into the teaching profession would pose a challenge. On this note, I avoided applying for jobs in the educational sector, which led to a different career path. Going into a different career path was time consuming and expensive as well. I was naive of what I wanted out of life; hence, I gave people the approval to make decisions on my behalf.

I lived a lie for a long time and compromised my self-worth to the point that I forgot my capabilities. As time passed, I began to speak the language of defeat, "I am not good enough, no one would hire me; I wish I looked like those I felt had a great appearance and accent." My life evolved outside of my true self, which affected my self-esteem to the point that I became a shadow of myself.

Some immigrants, like me, are also entangled in this viewpoint. I have seen doctors end their careers as cashiers, lawyers as cleaners, and bankers as cab drivers. The list is endless. They cheaply forget who they were before their journey as immigrants. It is easy to lose sight of your future when you empower people to define who you are. We forget our self-worth too soon and assume a position of defeat. When this occurs, it can lead to frustration and makes us want to give up on ourselves before others do.

The quest and reversal

Sometimes, it is easy to say what you want to become than who you are, especially if you have not discovered your self-worth. All your lifetime dreams and aspirations are embedded in you. Some are fortunate enough to know who they want to become from the onset, and they set out to actualize it early. On the other hand, some are not so lucky; they spend years exploring to uncover their true self.

It took me a long time to be able to debunk the limiting beliefs I had about myself. When I realized that my self-imposed limitations were not a true reflection of me, I changed. I began to speak confidence, strength, beauty, self-worth, and values. I read books about achievers, asked questions, and did research to help discover who I am. From my research, it was evident that I was more than my perceived level of growth. As an educator, it was apparent I could serve my world in different capacities, whether in starting a business, career transitions, personal development, book coaching, public speaking, and so forth.

Since the stakes of venturing into the teaching profession were high due to my accent and skin colour, I decided to set up a childcare learning centre where my teaching skills would be explored. This centre is designed to serve children between the ages of one to twelve years. In addition to owning the centre, I employ qualified teachers. As the director, my role is beyond teaching students; I also train educators from different parts of the world. Today, the centre has offered many student teachers a space to solidify their learning through the practicum program. The very thing that stood against me ended up setting the pace for my soaring. Don't allow situations to tell you otherwise. Devour your limitations.

Who are you?

Attaining greatness might be difficult if you don't understand yourself and your capabilities. One of the first questions people ask when they meet you for the first time in a gathering or anywhere is hello, "Who are you?" This is a conversation starter. After which, they may continue by asking, "What do you do?" These questions lay the foundation that ignites, builds, and sustains a conversation. Your ability to provide the correct response determines how far the conversation goes. The questions might appear simple yet challenging. It tells a mini story about you in a nutshell, so you need to be prepared to avoid being caught off-guard.

We are often confronted with it when we meet strangers. It is seldom for people to ask you directly, "Who are you?" A subtle way of asking could begin with, "Hello, what's your name?" As soon as you hear this, be prepared for the next,

"Tell me about yourself." This follow-up question is dependent on the environment. The purpose is for them to know and connect with you on another level. It may be difficult to escape it; however, it could become your selling point if answered correctly.

It is common for people to want to know what you do, and the reason for the things you do to understand your values. But sadly, most of us have no idea on how to respond because we genuinely don't know ourselves. We stutter and stammer because we have not taken the time to understand what we represent. The way we respond can expose our lack of self-awareness or confidence.

When next you are asked any of these questions, pay close attention to your response. What does your voice sound like? Do you feel excited? Do you keep it brief or try to change the subject as soon as possible? I have had my fair share of answering these questions. A few years ago, I had a strange experience when I met someone for the first time. She was older, confident, well dressed, and asked me what I do. I heard myself answer as if I was outside my body and realized how unsure I sounded. She nodded at me, but she did not take me seriously because my response wasn't convincing enough. It was a strange moment, and I realized the need to do some inner work!

Some time ago, someone asked me, "How do I know who I am?" One thing I usually say is this, "Take a retrospective of your childhood." What were the things you loved doing with ease before you became stripped as you grew older? Dig deep to check if you can salvage some of those attributes for your future reference. As I look back on my childhood days, I remember how I gathered my younger siblings to teach them how to read and write. Reflecting on those moments and where I am now, I am not surprised at my role as an educational consultant and teacher.

I remember a time in my junior school days when I wrote one of the best poems on "Harmattan." The teacher was impressed and amazed at my creativity. But somehow, along the way, I allowed my interest in writing to slip off. As time passed, I forgot the compliments I received as one of the best writers in my class back then.

In the search to discover who you are, venturing into new areas can be expensive. Some may try out new things to validate who they are. Investing so much in a business or education only to find out that it was a waste of time and resources can be discouraging. Imagine spending a fortune to become a surgeon and then, realizing that you cannot withstand the sight of blood. Switching to something new can be psychologically depressing and draining, especially after spending several years on it. Avoid being caught in that web of setback.

Impatient people usually jump from one career or business to another. Each time they indulge in this act, they end up starting from scratch. It is wise to know when to hold onto a career or business rather than exit. Those who drastically switch to something new rather than confront the issue always start afresh or begin at a lower level. Imagine someone who graduated in accounting and, after working for several years, suddenly decides to switch into becoming a pharmacist. That person will have to start all over from the ground level. Before embarking on any change, it is essential to think profoundly; remember the costs associated with it.

Honesty check

Have an honest discussion with yourself to find out where you stand in knowing yourself. If you can, I would like you to put this book down for a few minutes to have an honest conversation with yourself. Ask yourself these questions again, "What do I do?" and "What are the reasons for doing the things I do?" Try answering these questions aloud to warm up, and then move on to "Who am I?" Be sincere with your answers. How was your response? Were you able to answer with ease? How would you rate your performance on a scale of one to ten? Now, do you think you can comfortably sustain a conversation with anyone about yourself?

The first step to knowing who you are is to be truthful. Were you satisfied with your answers? If your answer is yes, congratulations on your ability to know who you are and why you do the things you do. On the other hand, if your answer is no, don't worry! You have nothing to lose; you can catch up. It only shows that you are on a journey to self-discovery. You can start by practicing how to answer these questions. Spending more time with yourself will expedite this process.

It is time to get to work. Pick up your pen and a notepad. Write down twenty things about yourself:

- What skills do you possess?
- What problems do people want you to solve for them?
- What do you love doing?

- What are the things that motivate you?
- If you could change the world or do any job right now, what would it be?

When we are cast into the world to answer, "Who am I?" It is scary, and often makes us to wonder: How on earth do I start defining my essence, the stuff that makes me who I am? If you can answer these questions truthfully, you will be amazed at what you will discover about yourself.

Yourself versus others

I loved watching movies and television series in my teenage years. I would do everything within my ability to ensure that my assigned tasks were completed before any of the series began. This handed me the time and freedom to sit glued to the television. Back then, narrating and giving a detailed account of the movies I watched was a huge part of me. Soon, this fantasy for movies became one of my biggest pastimes and way of relaxing. It felt harmless but time-consuming.

Several years have gone by, and I am still entrapped by some of these acts as an adult. Recently, I had the opportunity of attending a forty-five-minute seminar that was highly informative. A few days after, I could not stop talking about how great the speaker was and how well he delivered his presentations. I endlessly commented on the speaker's performance even when it was unnecessary. Maybe some of you can relate to this.

People indulge in things differently. To some, it could be as little as excessive sleep, or being involved with the wrong association, or spending a quality amount of time to talk about an artist or athlete they love. This lifestyle if not managed, could drive one to spending so much time and energy on others rather than themselves. People who engage in these acts may find it challenging to confidently sustain a five-minute conversation about themselves. This attitude can dampen growth if left unchecked.

People who are disproportionately motivated to know so much about others, without a clearly defined reason, may know only little about themselves. The quest to learn about others does not connote negativity; however, depending on the intent, it could. Aim to strike a balance; if you can invest the same amount of energy in learning about others to learn about yourself, then you are on the right path to self-discovery. Try to sit with yourself daily for at least five minutes to know who you are. In the past, I could hardly maintain that period of time with myself without distractions, and so I understand this perfectly well. Sitting alone with myself to reflect on who I am was quite a challenge.

It is interesting to note how easy it is to talk about and celebrate the achievements of others. But on the contrary, you may struggle to provide people with reasons to celebrate yours. We cheer, applaud, and dance to the victories of others while the world is patiently waiting to celebrate ours. Look inwards; what do you have that can positively influence your world? Enough of wallowing in someone else's world, it is time to show forth the greatness that lies dormant within you. Let what you know about yourself catapult you to a higher height. Remember, you can only live once, so take the leap and explore to discover who you are, now.

CHAPTER 2

Revealing You

> *There is no discovery without risk, and what you risk reveals what you value* —Jeanette Winterson

Revealing your inner self is not a game of chance; it is the beginning of self-revelation. Asking the right questions to the right person at the right time can reveal those hidden virtue you never knew existed within you. Sometimes, people see some of our attributes more than we do or even realize. Think about this, have you been complimented in a skill you never imagined you could excel at? There were times I felt shy and would do anything to avoid speaking in public. I remember how some of my friends would frequently remind me of how bold and eloquent I appeared. But I did not take it to heart back then. They saw those qualities in me long before I even knew I could speak in public. Apart from your hidden potentials being revealed by people, you can also unveil them on your own as well as unveil them in others.

My teenage son delights so much in using pictures of famous athletes for his social media profile. He calls them his idols. These pictures reveal and speak volumes of his interests. The other day, I engaged him in a conversation on why he chose those pictures, and these were his responses: "I admire them a lot and have great respect for them." He went on to add, "I look up to them, and would love to be like them in future." Those words were quite revealing of who they were and the level of influence they had on him. And I said to him, "I hope using them as your standard for growth will not limit you from revealing your own unique self." He is only sixteen with lots of untapped potentials.

It is not a bad idea to have role models that you can look up to, but be careful not to make their achievements stop you from becoming the best version of yourself. Some people make the success of others a benchmark for theirs. They are satisfied with achieving the same level of success as their idols and nothing more. Often, it is easy to want to be like someone else at the expense of who you ought to be.

Sometimes, I hear people make comments like, "In future, I would love to play basketball exactly like so-and-so," or, "I want to act like this actor or that actress when I grow older." They settle for the success level of others when they can indeed do better. Those you admire are there to inspire you to reach your maximum potential and not to limit your progress. Having them in your professional domain is beneficial and can challenge you to be your best self. For example, if you are a dancer, it would be preferable to have someone you admire and respect in that field for guidance. Their experiences can expose you to a new world of opportunities.

You matter

How often do you limit yourself? The desire to measure your achievement with that of others can distract you from attaining great heights. When I was as young as my sixteen-year-old son, I equally loved having role models. Like my son, my utmost desire was to have their exact kind of success. My life aspiration was centred on theirs. I didn't see the need to aim higher because there was no way I would have seen myself better than they were. As time went by, I realized that attaining their exact level of success was like a mirage. Eventually, I became exhausted with setting goals off someone else's standards and values, which were extremely frustrating.

Soon, I realized that having their exact kind of success was not a representation of me. I needed to believe in my unique abilities. During this time, I discovered that; everyone does not have to impact the world from a global stage. Whether you are a doctor or a cleaner, rich, or poor, you can create an impact in someone's life, right from where you are. It could be from your little corner, and in your unique way. The important thing is for you to be committed to serving those whose destinies are linked to yours. We all have our respective spheres of influence. Don't try to be like someone else. You don't have to occupy some sort of societal position to effect a change. Your shining is dependent on you. Refuse to close your ceiling; shatter the roof and dominate your space.

You've got it all

Most of us are conversant with looking up to our role models to the extent that; we sometimes forget to look at ourselves. For you to be able to showcase your true self, you need to learn how to look inward. This will enable you to bring to light what you have on your inside. You cannot run a race with your eyes fixed on someone else's goal rather than yours, you might end up in someone's lane if you do. This could make you miss the trophy, which is an expensive price to pay.

You have to continually stay in tune with your inner being to reveal yourself. Losing sight of your dreams and aspirations can happen swiftly, primarily when all your focus is centred on someone else. It is very natural to have an affinity for the people you admire. Most times, you are their greatest cheerleader and can help them advance their course. Consciously or unconsciously, you take delight in announcing their good deeds and sometimes share their achievements on different platforms. Imagine how far you went just to announce someone you admire to the world. It is excellent; there is no harm in doing that. What about you? How far have you gone for yourself?

Envision your attainment level, if you did a pinch of what you did for others for yourself, then you would have excelled. The irony is that most people are incredibly good at championing the course of others but find it difficult to do that for themselves. It is easy to showcase the people you admire but you find it difficult to showcase yourself.

The time has come to focus on yourself; you have worked hard enough for others. Go ahead and reveal that hidden potential for others to benefit from it. Look inwards, you have what it takes to be successful. Organizations and individuals are attracted to those who have unveiled their hidden potentials and are viewed as valuable assets. It is your responsibility to strategically reveal your talents for the world to feast on.

Situations and people reveal you

The desire to write a book came alive when a dear friend betrayed me. I was extremely hurt and wanted to put down my experiences in a book. That was the very first time I tried writing a book. But as I began to write, it was evident it came from a place of bitterness, anger, and brokenness. My words did not rest well with the messages, and I ended up trashing most of those words.

That experience marked the beginning of a new chapter in my life, which ignited a passion for writing and has led to where I am today. The seemingly rude behaviour from a friend and the issues that transpired brought out the author in me. Although it did not happen then; but it finally came true.

Sometimes, the negative behaviour from people or challenging situations happen to pave way for your soaring. Learn from any circumstance that tries to pull you down and refuse to be controlled by negativity and brokenness. Develop a flair for redesigning and repackaging issues that were designed to frustrate you. Create a message out of it, rebrand, and then use it to reveal your ideas to serve the world.

Stay true

There are lots of battles associated with staying true to one's self. Chapter One of this book highlights that the societal pressures inflicted on people, is one of such. This often forces them to redefine who they are, resulting in conformance with who they are not. Staying true will eliminate a life of lies and self-deceits. Living a life outside one's self is extremely conflicting. You need to be comfortable with the realization that being real is a gift you owe yourself to reveal your inner beauty. Loving and accepting yourself is critical at any phase in life, even when it's not in alignment with what you want. Life, some say, comes in different stages and being real is a prized virtue. Map out plans on how to make things fall in place.

Self-assessment

The self-assessment tool is critical in revealing a considerable part of you. Working as a facilitator for a non-profit organization brought to my knowledge the importance of this tool. During that time, one of my core duties was to advocate for families of low-income status. I assisted them in accessing donated clothing, food, subsidized shelter, and also set up accountability systems to manage their goals. This motivated and empowered most of them to actualize their dreams. Some gained admission to further their education; some found employment in their career paths, while others transitioned into new opportunities.

It was exciting to witness how majority of my clients lived their dreams. All their achievements were made possible through the Client Goal Management Scheme. A systematic accountability tool developed and implemented to empower clients to excel in their goals.

I derived so much satisfaction and fulfillment in my role as a facilitator. Providing support from the other end of the table was a great honour. It was a thing of joy to have been able to partake in their stories of struggles, pains, and tears. I do not take any of those moments for granted. The privilege of witnessing their transformational victories, seasons of celebration and laughter remains indelible.

Turning point

Despite all the achievements in working for my clients, I felt lost, realizing that there were some undeniable missing links in my goal setting. Living and embracing each day with the same routine was evident in my work ethic. It became glaring as time passed that helping others attain their goals came with ease, but I could not help myself achieve mine. There were no set goals to track my personal growth, except for the ones handed to me by the organization. In order to grow, it was critical to invest in my personal development, which I paid less attention to. Goal setting should be everyone's responsibility to monitor progress, no matter how small; create one.

The awareness of not investing enough time in my personal growth stung me hard. It dawned on me that I might wake up at the receiving end of the table one day. A place of receiving donated clothing, food, and subsidized shelter, just like most of my clients did. This gave me reasons to act; it was time to intentionally set and achieve my goals. Our actions today can positively or negatively affect our future tomorrow. At that moment, the fear of uncertainty stared at me right in the face.

Being sensitive to know when a season is over should not be overlooked. After carrying out an assessment, I knew the time had come to take a bow from the cooperate world. With a heart full of gratitude, I decided to throw in the towel and resigned from my nine to five job in pursuit of my dreams. In life, never leave what you can do right now for tomorrow because tomorrow may never come. Take the right action when your bones are full of strength.

My journey to becoming a pathfinder began in earnest with a few questions, and the answers became my turning point. The questions below are quick self-assessment tests to reveal who you are.

- Where do you see yourself in five or ten years from now; in your personal life, career, or business life?
- Do you know who you are and what you can do?
- What is your gifting?
- What are your strength and weaknesses?
- Can you comfortably tell the world who you are without gasping for breath?
- What skills do you possess, both acquired and internal?
- What problems can you comfortably and uncomfortably solve?
- Who do you think could benefit from your gifting?
- Where can you find them?
- How can you serve them in any capacity?
- Is there anyone you would need to speak to for guidance?

- If yes, who can you talk to for direction and clarity?
- Are you ready to take action with what you have discovered about yourself?

You don't have to provide answers to all the questions right away. The results can lead you to the next level of growth. Take some time to think through before embarking on any action. In my case, the answers I derived at made me restless and held me accountable. What I gleaned from those self-inquiry questions drove me to work on myself. It triggered a desire to reveal my inner strength as well as chase after my personal development.

Feedback

Feedback is an essential piece of growth. I got better at writing as a result of the feedback from friends and family members. Even though my writing began early in life, I wasn't completely sold out to it. I spent most time imagining how no one would read or purchase my work if I eventually did write. Nothing would have made me to envision writing a book that is powerful enough to captivate readers. But here I am today with a book, Be Your Pathfinder, right in your hands. It became a reality because of feedback. Those feedbacks handed me the audacity to make this book a dream come true.

Some feedback may be painful to accept, especially when it negates expectations. However, to accomplish its purpose, one must keep an open mind; and be willing to accept people's viewpoints. This can expedite growth. Feedback exposes you to a world of new learning. Accept it in good faith, whether good or bad. It could be used as a yardstick to improve areas of deficiencies. When giving one, it is normal for some people to be biased while some are not. Overall, feedback can result in clarity if it is effectively managed. It provides us with the strategy on how to implement plans for our advancement as well as monitors our progress. We must design an enabling environment to ask and receive one.

Strength and weakness

> *Success is achieved by developing our strengths, not by eliminating our Weaknesses — Marilyn Vos Savant*

I lived in denial of the strengths that are embedded in my weaknesses for a long time. Public speaking was the last thing in my mind. The fear of being ridiculed took hold of me. The thought that no one would show up or listen to me overwhelmed me in my head. These further intensified my phobia for speaking or even wanting to step on any stage. The fear redefined and framed my personality and made me withdrawn. I would sit anywhere in a room, but not anywhere near the front. The mere sight of an empty seat in the front row made me tremble. If sitting in front made me panic this much, imagine how disoriented it would be to speak in front of an audience from a stage.

I told those who cared to listen; how I was born to rule from behind-the-scenes just to cover up my phobia and I was comfortable with that. Like me, some people have missed out on life-changing opportunities because they underestimated their abilities. It took feedback and encouragement to see and draw strengths from my weaknesses. And now, what I believed as one of my most significant flaws, public speaking, turned out to be one of my biggest strengths.

Whenever you feel insufficient, pause, and think about a time when you felt incapable of doing the things you are currently doing. The ability to excel in your weaknesses just as your strengths is in you. Life is not always about capabilities, even though it has a way of making us rely on our strengths rather than our weaknesses.

Sooner or later, you will end up realizing that some of those perceived weaknesses are your most substantial strengths. Nobody has it all figured out; perfection is merely unattainable. Not doing certain things now is not an indication of weakness; it might not be the right time. Before now, I exhibited a total lack of confidence in my vocabulary to coin the right words for a book.

In the past, I felt intimidated when people say that they are born writers. This is different for me. My writing was born out of a strong desire to perfect my writing skills. Most importantly, my past experiences brought out the beauty of writing in me. Some indeed have talents; however, all good and experienced writers achieve success through hard work and perseverance. I have long realized that there is no easy way to a writer's life. If one has a desire to write, then they must doggedly follow through the process. This is the way writers are wired, and as one, that is how I follow through.

Revealing your authentic self will never be complete without your strengths and weaknesses. Our successes and failures are all interwoven to form who we are. Celebrate your weaknesses as much as you celebrate your strengths.

There are moments when embracing your flaws can elevate you.

I remember the first time a request was sent for me to feature in a promotional video clip. It was a marketing advertisement for a previous organization I had worked for. On receiving the request, my first response was a loud "Noooooo!" I bluntly told the crew how they had chosen the wrong candidate for the role. To further worsen the situation, I had only about forty-five minutes to prepare for the interview before the camera started rolling. Despite my loud protests, I was persuaded to try, and I reluctantly did it, against my inclination.

In clear but simple terms, I narrated how lives have been transformed through our services. I also mentioned how most of our clients rose from subsidized living to owning their first homes, got jobs, went back to school, and more. Some of these clients did chose to say thank you by giving back to the community. Their once lonely and isolated lives were replaced with great new connections. Above all, they found their path to success and were living a fulfilled life. The session was concluded with a brief recap of how our services transformed and are still changing lives.

Nothing would have informed me how well the interview went. I was sure without a doubt that I blundered, or at least, that was my impression. This made me tensed and restless after the session. It seemed as if my best was not good enough. But to my utmost surprise, when the production came out, some people were touched and broke down in tears. Knowing that the little services we rendered made such a huge impact was amazing.

In a similar event, I was appointed to give a speech for an annual general meeting and was persuaded. Again, it attracted the same reaction as the previous. I was amazed at the feedback; some said, "You inspire me," while others said, "You were born for the stage." I was in shock at how my words could positively penetrate the hearts of people.

I have learned to draw a lot of life-changing lessons from past experiences. You see, sometimes, the very things you are afraid of might equally be scared of you. Be intentional and stage a war against any belief that is out to stop you from revealing your true self.

CHAPTER 3

Transformational Growth

> *In any given moment we have two options: to step forward into growth or step back into safety* —Abraham H. Maslow

In the first chapter of this book, we dwelt extensively on exploring to discover. Now that you have a better understanding of yourself, it is time to begin the process of personal development. Growth is possible when it is aligned with self-discovery. Make a conscious effort to ensure that who you are connected with your identity to avoid drifting into confusion.

This chapter aims to equip the readers with the knowledge and understanding of investing in their development. This brings about stability in life as well as reinforces your identity. Life is all about growth. We are either growing older and developing or stagnating intellectually. Everybody grows, whether physically or mentally. There should be no compromise when it comes to our physical and intellectual growth. Depending on our cycle of life, we are either growing taller, bigger, or shrinking. We age as time passes. Development is synonymous with internal transformation and is noticeable in our outward conduct. Occasionally, I often hear words like, "He is twenty years old but still acts like a child." Although the person in this scenario is an adult, his mental state is likened to that of a child.

Some form of growth occurs naturally; they are bestowed upon us at birth, like our height, hair, nails, and so on, while some require constant activation. For example, no one is born a doctor or surgeon. To become one, they must undergo a series of intellectual development to attain such heights. Even though our growth and development may appear to be similar, however, they play distinctive roles at different intervals of our existence. Growth and development are expected to happen in every sphere of our lives for us to function at our maximum capacity. Very often, we focus so much on our physical growth than our internal development. Some people grow externally but struggle to develop internally.

I had a friend in my elementary school days that overgrew and looked more matured than I was. At fourteen years of age, she was often mistaken for an adult just by her appearance. But whenever she spoke, the immaturity in her showed up. Even though she looked matured, her mental, social, and emotional conducts were not fully developed to handle maturity. In this circumstance, the contrast between growth and development is very evident.

Development should be consistent in our journey to success. Most people who work in the corporate world are usually exposed to a professional development plan by their employers. Some entrepreneurs sponsor themselves through the process, while some do not see the need for it. Professional and personal developments are critical subject that should be given adequate attention. In order to advance, you need to put a plan in place to develop regularly.

Broaden your horizons

There is no point in getting to know who you are and what you can do without wanting to broaden your horizon. The world is continuously evolving, and we also need to change with the times and seasons. Doing the same thing over and over and expecting to get a different result is not feasible. Avail yourself the opportunity to learn something new, learning should be a lifelong affair, and there is no end to it. No knowledge is wasted; they improve and add substantial value to your worth.

Building on your present level of growth strategically positions you to opportunities. Sometimes, depending on our financial status, we rely on others for our development. Some people in the corporate world get stuck with this attitude. They get to a point where they are reluctant to invest in themselves, but instead expect their organization to do so on their behalf. It is essential to move past this stage; if nobody enrolls you for a training, enroll yourself. If you get into the routine of depending on someone else for your growth, you might end up waiting for too long. Be committed and responsible to issues that affect your advancement.

The same goes for entrepreneurs, some believe that having a business of their own exempts them from investing in their growth. They may be tempted to think that they no longer need further development because they are in charge. Nevertheless, being the boss of your business should not deter you from investing in your progress. When you invest in yourself, you are investing in your business and career. This broadens your horizon and advances your expertise.

Clarity

Just by discovering who you are is not enough to accomplish your goals. It is only the beginning of the journey. Self-development shows you the big picture. Clarity leads to growth when you align yourself with your "what" and your "how."

Your "what" is having sight of the big picture, which is the end goal. Your "how" is mapping out a plan to achieve your "what." Your "what" must be in sync with your "how" for productivity to be achieved. People who are not prudent may have a great "what" with an obscured "how." For example, wanting to be a teacher without going through the process is not enough to make you one. Until you pay attention to the process, your vision will be scattered in different directions. Clarity helps you understand how to follow through the process of greatness.

Self-reliance

The way to confidently defend who you are without second-guessing is to be knowledgeable in what you do. When you are in tune with self-reliance, it allows you to grow exponentially. People usually believe in those who are confident in their expertise. This is an indication that a person is knowledgeable.

Self-reliance is a vital piece of carving a successful path in life. It does not just happen; it takes repetitive learning and practice to get there. You don't become an expert by doing things only once. The act of doing something repeatedly reinforces understanding, which gives you the courage to undertake any task in your area of specialty. Partaking in regular self-development sharpens and improves your confidence.

As an educational consultant, I have had the privilege of seeing children and teachers transform in a short period of time. Most of them came into the environment incredibly nervous, shy, and afraid of taking risks. At first, some children may struggle with the use of materials like scissors, pencils, and some others. But over time, with practice and repetition, they end up mastering the art of self-sufficiency. This practice helps boost their confidence. The same thing happens with some new teachers; they may start shy and unsure of what to do or say initially in class, but eventually become exceptionally good at what they do. Self-reliance becomes a reality when you allow yourself to develop on a repeated basis.

Focus

Research reveals that as of today, the average attention span of humans is eight seconds. This is shorter than that of a goldfish. With this finding, there is a need for us to discipline ourselves in order to be productive. In a world full of distraction, societal pressures, and technology overdose, we need self-control to stay on track. There is an ongoing battle between spending our time in productive and unproductive activities.

Our focus is constantly challenged with our minds wandering for what to do. The onus to focus on things that will trigger growth lies within us. Distraction is a choice; one can choose to focus or to be distracted. It is common for people to start a thing and not complete it. Some started school and never finished, while some started to write and were unable to complete it due to lack of focus.

Broken focus ultimately leads to fragmented results. Some cannot complete a task because they are exposed to more than what they can handle. Dealing with several tasks at the same time causes additional stress, which can streamline growth. Your body is not designed to do everything; engaging in everything will make you end up nowhere. Those who carry excessive tasks eventually burn out and underperform. Like the saying goes, "Jack of all trades, master of none." It is wise to handle limited tasks that you are sure of executing perfectly well than to get entangled with many and end up struggling. After all, it is often said, "anything worth doing is worth doing right." — Hunter S. Thompson

Focus is like the vehicle that drives you to your destination. To effectively and efficiently grow, managing your attention span is a prerequisite. Undivided attention is required for excellent results in any assigned job. It is time to silence the noise around you, uproot all the distractions, fix your gaze on the big picture, keep moving, and don't stop until you have added virtue to who you are.

Starting and completing this book was not easy. There were times I wanted to opt-out due to numerous distractions and the pressures of life. It took discipline, resilience, and focus to concentrate. Self-development enhances focus and empowers you to stand strong in the face of adversities. It is one of the core ingredients for your advancement, and it motivates you to work with a target in mind.

Past experiences

Experience comes in different shades; negative or positive. Depending on your viewpoint, either of those has the power to develop or tear you down. They can affect your decision-making and shape your thought process. Experience is often termed as the best teacher. A person who has gone through the pain of losing a loved one knows the exact spot where the shoe pinches rather than someone who only watches from afar. It feels harmless to judge a man for allowing his child to play freely, until you realize how broken that family has been over the death of a wife and mother. Experiences have a way of making us do better.

In my second book, "Lessons From Trailblazer," people who experienced hardship fought hard to live above failure. They were able to carve a successful path in what they do due to what they have been through in life. I have few friends who went through tough moments to survive in their childhood days. They lost their parents early in life, which made them struggle through school. When they eventually got a job or started a business, they were determined to succeed against all odds. Their encounter with hardship served as a catalyst for growth and framed them into becoming pathfinders.

Career-wise, some experience comes with consistency in your role and exposes you to grow professionally. Spending nine years as a pilot is different from someone who barely spent two months in the same profession. The person with only two months of experience will have to undergo a series of professional and personal development to be able to navigate through turbulence times. It takes years to develop some skills and expertise.

Few people have been instrumental in my growth; I learn from those who have gone ahead of me, and from different sources. These sources include: reading books, exploring different information platforms, and being coached regularly. Great accomplishment always stirs me to improve. I also know that some people look up to me for their growth just like I do to others. These people challenge me to take action in developing myself daily. I believe people will also look up to them to be inspired if they work hard enough. Everyone, irrespective of their levels and status should have a way of inspiring someone to grow and become the best version of themselves.

It is often believed that you grow when you surround yourself with like-minded people or highflyers. Some say, "Variety is the spice of life." We need different levels of associates to excel, both the high achievers, and those who are yet to become one. Surrounding yourself with only high achievers is excellent, but remember those who are on a journey to attaining theirs because we need each other to grow. It is great to advance with the support of highflyers, but don't deprive those without a successful track record, the opportunity to develop and grow through you. This is called the cycle of life. You learned from others; it is wisdom to position yourself for others to learn from you.

There is no point surrounding yourself with only those who can inspire you to grow, without having people you can equally motivate to grow. This is a defective concept. Life consists of giving and receiving. Receiving without giving can lead to intellectual obesity. Helping others reach their full potential does not diminish your worth; it only makes you a master in what you do. It increases your value and circle of influence.

Lessons from the Libyan War

Living in Libya was an eye-opener to understand that the grass is not always greener on the other side. It was my first international experience outside my home country, Nigeria. I thought everything would fall into place upon my arrival, so I travelled to Libya on a cross-posting without having any aims or goals in mind and I embraced each day as it unfolded. My new norm was to hang out with friends over coffee and visiting historical sites just to keep busy. I had enough time at my disposal but took it for granted.

Looking back at those years, it would be fair to say I lived a life of emptiness, self-centeredness, and lack of focus. Instead, I have chosen to turn it into a life of learning. Maybe if I wasn't exposed to that lifestyle, the motivation to be where I am today would not have been feasible. Some experiences prepare you for the next chapter of your life.

In February 2011, the war in Libya was a wakeup call. My high expectations of living a life of luxury came crashing in a twinkle of an eye and forced me to view life with a different lens as I took stock of my lifestyle. Tough seasons have a way of humbling and making you think twice. Even though the war brought an end to my living there, however, it marked the beginning of my quest for personal development.

It was during the war I realized the very essence of my living. As we departed, I realized that life is one of the greatest gifts of all times and for it to be meaningful; it must be steered in the right direction. I left Libya with a sigh of relief, leaving behind all the material possessions I had acquired.

The journey out of Libya came with mixed feelings. I was leaving behind a country I once thought would bring me peace and satisfaction but now lie in ruins due to war. The trip out of Libya was horrifying. I hate to make this confession, but that is simply the truth. It was a turbulent trip loaded with severe sea storms. The fierceness of the storm caused me to doubt if we would survive. Out of fear of the unexpected, I kept my eyes shut for most part of the journey, so as not to witness the capsizing of the boat. In the process, I slept off at different intervals.

Faint murmurs and heavy throttling sound from the engine awakened me. The possibility of everyone drowning flooded my thought. When I opened my eyes, what I saw baffled me, and brought tears to my eyes. With a blurry vision, I could see very tiny houses from afar. The more I struggled to see, the more difficult it was as my eyes became swollen with tears. What happened next can never be comprehended; the shouts of joy and tears that erupted in the boat, could not be contained.

A journey of about forty-five minutes on air ended up taking over ten hours at sea. The boat finally came to a halt.

Phew! What a relief. At last! We made it to the shore alive despite the severity of the war and sea storm. Even though living in Libya at first appeared to lack substantial purpose; however, it ended up giving me a few life lessons that I will never exchange for anything. I returned empty-handed but alive, I remain thankful to God for sparing my life and that of my family.

Those experiences taught me that life is filled with uncertainties; nothing in life is permanent. The life lessons from Libya have been a great pillar and anchor point to my growth. This is where my attention and craving for self-development all began. Sometimes, I look back at those memories in tears. But through it all, I have learned to turn those experiences into learning opportunities and advancement.

Everyone has experiences to draw from, they are our life-time companion as humans, and transpires naturally. As you sail through life, you will continually encounter different moments, both good and bad. What you do with those encounters will determine the outcome. In times of difficulties, count it all joy and try to twist it around for your good. Use your experiences to map out a plan to excel. How you navigate through those seasons could be the game-changer for your breakthrough. Through my experience in Libya, I now have a better understanding that living without intention and purpose only leaves you empty. And time not invested wisely can never be regained. My narrow escape from the war will always remain one of the most significant boosts to my professional and personal development.

CHAPTER 4

The Game-Changer

Game-changers are those who rule the affairs of their lives. They don't leave their stage for others to run the show. These people know what it means to take charge of their future. They understand that life is not a game of chance. It is their responsibility to make decisions and stand by it. Anyone can be a game-changer by virtue of their creative ideas and analytical thinking. As one, you can initiate a revolution based on your provocative thought pattern.

Life will always consist of hurdles, but how you manoeuvre through them can alter the narrative of your setbacks for good. Take the necessary action to swing your struggles in the right direction. People who are pacesetters in their area of specialty are often remembered as solution makers. They have a stimulating mindset that can keep up with the events of the season. These people carve a path for themselves and for others to follow.

After reading Chapters One to Three, I believe you are fired up to lead the change movement in every area of your life. Develop a blueprint on how to effect a change to enhance your progress. You can start by writing out your vision, mission statement, and values. Redefine, rebrand, and reposition yourself to create impact; the era of playing small is over. This understanding will help you evaluate the viability of your systems and structures. Seize every opportunity that comes your way; don't let them slip by.

The ability to provide solutions to problems makes you standout. Sometimes, challenges show up to open doors of breakthroughs. Sadly, those who are meant to shine and make a name in the face of opposition shrink into their shell when the going gets tough.

Identifying and complaining about a problem are the most natural things for anyone to do. Often, only a few see and seize opportunities in challenges. The world is searching for those who can identify problems and offer solutions. People who are supposed to be at the forefront often end up in the back seat of life. Their inability to swing issues into stepping-stones often causes them to struggle.

Some are regularly making waves and creating impact with the very thing you are busy complaining about. Quit complaining, it will take you nowhere. Some people have become billionaires from the very problem you identified and complained but did not proffer solution to it. The difference between those who complain and those who take action is that those who take action end up changing the narrative of events for good.

From my observation, those who complain appear to have excellent ideas on problem solving but don't act on those ideas. For instance, their concern might be over the poor packaging of a product or a speaker's poor performance. Do you know, these people might have a tip or two on how to revamp the speaker's skills or packaging products that attract customers? Rather than complaining from the sideline, they can create a course on making speakers ace in their presentations? Or on quality packaging that sells? When next you find yourself complaining, just breathe, have a rethink, and then ask yourself, "How can I solve the problem? What can I do to offer solution?" The answers in the "How" and "What" will give you a clue.

It is possible to have great ideas, talk about it, share it with friends and loved ones, but never take a step towards making it a reality. But as soon as someone else ventures into that terrain, you beat yourself up, and worry over the very stuff you delighted in only talking about. If you have excellent ideas, why waste it? There is no perfect time to put your ideas to work other than now. Go ahead and take action.

It might not be feasible to provide solutions to all the problems you identify. However, you can pick and choose at least one problem you feel comfortable enough to explore and solve. You can collaborate with others to solve the problem if it is a huge one or if you are not confident enough to work alone. It is not necessary to have everything figured out before taking action. Nothing can stop you, except you, if you are truly set to impact your world, you will find a way to do so. As the common phrase goes, "Where there is a will, there is a way." Refuse to succumb to a life of complaint.

Fail to rise

Our rising is sometimes dependent on our failures. Being a game changer can bring you in collision with it. Henry Ford failed many times before he succeeded, and today, he is known as the father of automobiles. Failure is not final; it can be redefined when you understand why you started and why you failed. The purpose of starting a thing empowers you in the face of adversity. According to Bill Sunday, "More men fail through lack of purpose than lack of talent." The ability to rise above failures will hand you a trophy at the end. Until you take time to understand the reason for doing what you do, you will continue to shift base whenever you come face to face with failure.

Giving up because of failure is like abandoning a seed you planted to die. When you chose to forgo a project due to failure and move to something new, it could result in starting from scratch. This could be likened to replanting a new seed, which often takes time to grow. Interrupting the process of growth takes you back to the beginning because growth does not happen overnight. Changing base or running away from failures is like running away from your shadow. This act will only prolong your meeting with success. Before moving to start something new, it is vital to have a valid reason for the shift. Confront your failures because you will most likely overcome what you confront.

People who rose to stardom fought hard to break free from giving up. They made failure a place of rest and re-launched again. Henry Ford captured it nicely: "A failure is just a resting place. It is an opportunity to begin again more intelligently." Failure is not a sign of weakness, in some cases, the only way to succeed is to fail. Think about a time when you thought you failed at a project, and then, it turned out to be a success. People who don't give up are those who become sought after.

When you think of quitting because of setbacks, think about Abraham Lincoln, who left for war as a captain and returned with the lowest military rank, a private. He again cuddled failure with numerous failed business ventures. As if that was not enough, in his political field, he failed on several occasions before he finally became the President of the United States of America. Tenacity and consistency are crucial to carving a successful path. Being a game changer does not take place overnight; it comes with a prize. You must be willing to sacrificially serve with your time, energy, and other available resources.

Some failures can expose you to self-doubt and make others doubt you as well. It is even more disturbing when the people you know, especially your friends, family members, colleagues, or acquaintances doubt you. They may find it difficult to believe in you again because of past failures. This experience can be very agonizing. Be courageous enough to keep taking more strides; even if the whole world questions your abilities and misunderstands you; refuse to doubt and misunderstand yourself. Choose to focus on the big picture. If you stand firm, you will be celebrated, despite all the storms. I read somewhere that Michael Caine failed to a point that his headmaster told him, "You will be a laborer all your life." and eventually, Caine labored his way to two Academy Awards."

I have also failed in my own little way at many things. The first business I started in my home country came with so much hardship right from inception. Barely after I began, I suffered severe losses as a result of incessant theft. The number of times my business premises was broken into was outrageous. Each theft came with a huge financial setback and dilemma.

I was at a crossroad of whether to quit or continue with the business. Despite the frustrations and predicament, I made a conscious effort to carry on. That business arena is still viable in my absence and has been in operation for over ten years. I call it the generational business premise because it has been handed down to different family members for different business intent and is still serving its purpose.

Even though I may have failed initially, but now, looking back, I feel honoured that the business premise is still waxing strong. This would not have been possible if I had given up because of the incessant theft, and financial instability. Life is all about risk, sometimes you lose, and sometimes you win. The ability to bring out the best in any circumstance is what sets you apart.

Timeline

There is nothing infinite on earth. People who are result driven cannot afford to work without a timeline. For a goal to be termed complete, it has to be time driven. Nearly everything we do is tied to it. No one can work, go to school, stay young, live with parents, or children, forever. Timeline is like a report card to check our level of advancement.

Everyone needs it for guidance. It measures progress and setbacks and tells you when to apply speed and slow down, and if you are working hard or not. It manages expectations, for instance, before I started writing this book, I had a deadline in mind for the completion. I believe before you started reading this book, you did set aside time to complete it. I also know that some people will not finish reading this book due to time constraints.

Scheduling provides a snapshot of where you stand and where you need to be with tasks. It tracks growth and gives a clear picture of where adjustments are necessary. In as much as scheduling is essential, sometimes, it comes with setbacks. It is critical to apply caution when working towards meeting deadlines; notably, in difficult situations where delays are unavoidable. A little tweak here and there can ensure quality. Understand when to adjust pressing deadlines to accommodate quality performance if the need arises. Substituting quality over timelines can jeopardize an entire project.

I once had a tailor sew a dress for me to wear for a friend's wedding. He was prompt with the delivery date, but the sad part was that the dress came out undersized. It was not suitable for the occasion. I asked to know what went wrong; he apologized and said he was in a hurry to meet the deadline. He compromised quality just to meet the deadline. I ended up not wearing that dress, I completely lost it. It does not harm to tweak timelines by a day or two to enhance quality. People celebrate quality over quantity. Timeline with excellence is a great way to stay ahead of the game.

Success

Success begins with you; it does not just happen. It is a combination of many things; hard work, determination, focus, commitment, failure, consistency, and the list goes on. It's the sum of progressive steps towards attaining goals. It is not a one size fits all; it differs from person to person.

Everyone defines success in a language that suits them. Do you want to succeed? Look inward; what can you see? In the words of Steve Goodier, "The first secret to success: Believe in Yourself. Nothing changes in your life until you believe you can do things that are important to you." Success begins with believing in yourself. You need to believe in who you are and what you can do before anyone else will think of believing in you.

The only reason we do most of the things we do is to succeed: Why do you wake up early to go to work? Why are you into business, or why do you go to school? Why did I write this book? The answer is noticeably clear and straightforward; we engage in all of these because we want to succeed; if not, there won't be a need to do them. I am yet to see a person who is not interested in being successful. Even though everybody's desire is to become successful in their chosen endeavour; however, not everyone will work hard enough to earn it. If success were to be stumbled upon, most people would be successful, but it is a combination of hard work, commitment, and many more.

Success is far from wishes, neither is it free for all. It comes with a price tag. Great people give up some of life's pleasures to get to where they want to be. To some, it may be exchanging a few hours of sleep to study or getting a task completed; while to others, it could be denying themselves of some social events. Any of these can make one a game-changer.

Actors and actresses don't fall from the sky to steal the show. Before they attain such height, they must have invested sleepless nights to work hard from behind-the-scenes with script edits, repeat performances, and memorizing parts of the script. Some productions may take as long as over a year, if not more, to create a quality production. The stake involved for them to pull a grand performance is high because they are always expected to excel.

Discipline is one of the most important core ingredients to success. People who lack discipline would most likely end in failure. My husband often uses this phrase, "Show me a man who lacks discipline, and I will show you a man who is far from success." This man will require discipline to wake up early and to stay focus on getting tasks done in order to be productive.

Pay close attention to how you deal with success and failure. Often, past accomplishments could be our biggest obstacle to future progress. Past failures; could also be instrumental to our success. Some of my greatest achievements that were not carefully managed resulted in my worst falls, and some falls gave me a push for success. However, I have grown from both experiences.

It takes discipline to handle success. From my experience, I have seen people who lack boundaries on how they spend time. Their desire is to please or satisfy people against their wishes just to maintain the relationship. They try to respond to nearly every request thrown at them. This lifestyle cripples efficiency and productivity. I acted this way in the past, but I have grown over the years and have learned to say no to certain things. It's okay to desire to respond to every request thrown at you, especially from close allies. Nevertheless, you must know when to draw boundaries for the sake of your advancement and sanity.

You were not created to serve or say yes to everybody, neither were you created to serve just a handful of people such as your immediate family, friends, or colleagues. Saying yes to everyone does not always yield a meaningful impact. You don't have to jeopardize your health by running in circles just to please people on their terms.

Don't expend your energy on only a few people when you can indeed reach and serve the world with what you've got. You are more prominent than where you are and what you are currently doing. Be bold enough to step out, the world is patiently waiting for your manifestation. It's far better to arrive at your end goal with few friends; than to please everyone and lose sight of where you are going and eventually end nowhere. There is dignity in a "Yes" and "No" response. Either of those two statements can plot a graph for a productive lifestyle.

CHAPTER 5

The Power of a Coach

> *A good coach can change a game. A great coach can change a life* —John Wooden

Coaches are like sounding cymbal; they help you overcome obstacles and create a mental picture for a positive mindset shift. Most experiences that imprint a memorable and lasting impression are those with one-on-one encounters. They leave us with lessons that stick with us for a lifetime. Very often, we tend to remember how we felt during those encounters, and it takes a great coach to make that happen. A great coach celebrates your high and low seasons. They go the extra mile to de-escalate your pains, aches, defeats, fears, tears, and doubts. Their role is influential in helping you achieve your set goals.

Have you ever seen a soccer or basketball coach during a game? They are usually very restless and find it extremely hard to sit still just for a minute. These coaches pace and run from one end to the other while sometimes screaming the players' names from the sideline with instructions on how to defeat their opponent. It is quite difficult for them to take their eyes off the pitch until the game is over. If they are fortunate enough to win the match, their reaction after victory tells the story of how much passion they have for their role. They run, jump, and sometimes take off their ties, cap, suits, and shoes to celebrate their victory. It is even more heartbreaking to watch how some of them break down and weep publicly during defeat. It goes a long way to reveal that their hearts and souls are in what they do, and they are doggedly committed to their role. It shows their in-depth love for the team. They win and lose together.

As I cast my mind back, I remember my experience with a coach, which later led to the completion of this book. "Yes you!" She pointed in my direction as she repeated those words. "Yes you! You won!" Those words came from a lady who later became my coach; I won a door prize and a free coaching session. All this happened at a women's conference in 2018. That door prize became a springboard to the various layers of my attainments.

Her first question to me was: What are your goals in life? And I answered, "To complete my book." Without a doubt, I knew it was time to complete the writing of my first book. My dream has always been to inspire people through writing. Before then, I had written many pages that could possibly make up a book. But the completion process was one of my biggest challenges. At this point, it was apparent that I needed some external help to hold me accountable to get the work done, and I found one in my coach. She came into my life at the right time and season.

It all began with a free coaching session I won at the conference, which later evolved into a voluntarily paid session. This was necessary to accomplish my goal of writing a book. I have grown to realize that some free stuff has a way of holding one captive and could potentially limit progress. It could also lead to a stale commitment if not checked. Investing in your development makes you committed and a stakeholder. I opted for the paid option because I was thirsty for results. The evidence of investing in a coach is right in your hands, my book, "Be Your Pathfinder."

It was in working with a coach that I discovered the power of a positive mindset, the wonders of accountability, and meeting targets. My attainments in writing would have been incomplete without a great coach, and today, I am a game-changer and an author. I believe everyone needs a coach; someone to walk them through obstacles.

Roadblocks are inevitable and are bound to occur; whenever you meet one, confront it. Seek help from those you trust or look up to when the going gets tough. It may be a coach, a mentor, or anyone who can help you manoeuvre through the difficulties. Do not feel embarrassed or shy to reach out when you are stuck. Be humble enough to learn from those who have gone through that route before you.

Life is a choice and moving beyond stagnation is also a choice. Avoid procrastination; it leads nowhere. Anything is possible if you set your mind on it. Some people, out of necessity, will require support to reach their targets. If by any means you decide to work with a coach along the way, here are a few tips to guide you:

- Know what you want from the onset; be clear on your goals
- Pause and review if you are a good fit for your coach. If yes, carry on, but if no, make a change
- Be flexible; there is nothing written in stone. Some goals could be tweaked for maximum results as you progress
- Understand your role and that of your coach: both roles are distinct: your coach is not there to do the work for you but to guide you
- Establish a clearly defined boundary
- Eliminate assumptions by asking questions for clarity
- Work with timelines to enable you meet your goals
- Always check-in if unsure of tasks
- Honour appointments; if unable to show up, give a heads up
- Don't take things for granted; respect the terms and conditions
- Get the work done with all commitment and determination
- Review your progress with your coach at every step of the way
- Pick up yourself whenever you fall behind schedule and celebrate accomplishments
- Know when the cycle is over and call it a day with a heart full of gratitude

Do not leave your destiny in someone else's hands when you know that accomplishing your goal is your sole responsibility. It is crucial to learn how to take charge of your life. Set your priorities right to avoid conflicts when working with your coach. Stay focus through the process, avoid distractions, have fun when necessary, enjoy every moment. Most of all, know when to capture and celebrate successful moments, whether big or small, because they don't happen often. Be confident enough to believe in yourself.

Social media: a web of distraction

Social media can change the terrain of our lives, depending on its usage. The world, as it stands right now, is saturated with so much information. This information, if not responsibly managed could become a source of distraction and hindrance to our growth. We live in an era where we go to sleep and wake up with different mediums of information stuck by our bedside. Some have become almost inseparable from their phones. A vast number of people are addicted to excessive information, according to research. These people embrace any information that crosses their path without validating them. They have perpetually made themselves a dumping ground for all sorts of information. These are all distractions that could potentially lead one astray from progressing.

Nowadays, news about the world is at your fingertip. You don't have to reside in a country to get firsthand information about any unfolding events in that country. With your phones, tablets, or electronic devices, you can tour the world at will. Ingesting excessive information can end in what I call information constipation; it is vital to pick and chose amid surplus information. Apply only the ones that are relevant and discard the unwanted ones. Receiving and hoarding information that can lead to your advancement should be discouraged.

Imagine a person who spends most of his time surfing social media for pleasure at the expense of preparing for a job interview. He showed up on the day of the interview without a complete document. When asked, his response was that he forgot to read through the section that required him to come with his documents. He lost out on a vital opportunity that would have added substance to his life due to his inability to control his vast appetite for social platform.

Browsing the internet has come to stay, and one needs to develop a strategic plan on how to stay focused. When using social space, it can be frustrating when an advert automatically pops up without warning; this could result in a waste of time. You can make social media work to your advantage, or you might end up working for it. In order to stay focused, develop strategies to minimize distractions, set up a timer to monitor and track your level of usage, stick to your priorities when browsing, and if possible, block or un-follow any unwanted sites.

It's no news that we live in a world that is prevalent with the use of social media. The effects are evident in both young and old. The truth is that it is here to stay and will get more sophisticated with time. Keep in mind that two things will always happen with the use of this tool: it will either elevate or destroy you. It is time to wage war against distraction when accessing social media. Excessive indulgence in the use of technology will stop you if you don't stop it.

Some of us cannot do without it as it is an essential piece to what we do daily. It is a hub for many things; the good, the bad, and the ugly, and we see all kinds of people on it. This tool has the power to make people fail or succeed. I have made friends and great connections on this platform. I have learned from the old and young, the wise and unwise. Like some, I have laughed and cried and made my fair share of mistakes as well as learned from it. On the social space, I have seen that life is not only for the perfect. Everyone has a part to play and something to offer. Therefore, position yourself to be a game-changer when using it.

Self-care

> *By taking care of myself, I have so much more to offer the world than I do when I'm running on empty —Ali Washington*

Most people often take self-care for granted. They give less attention to its importance and yet want to be at their peak performance. Not having enough rest is a silent killer to all your goals and aspirations. Don't underestimate the hazard that stress can cause in your overall growth. Productivity is at its maximum when you are well-rested. Being a game-changer cannot be complete without a proper self-care.

Let's carry out a little self-care analysis test:

- First, pick a note pad and pen,
- Next, write your first seven most important priorities
- Then, read it aloud to yourself.
- Circle your number one, two and three priorities on the list
- Read it aloud again to yourself

Now, let's carry out a reality check with the answers you provided on your list of priorities:

- Did you include self-care?
- Pause for a moment; what number does your self-care belong to in the list?
- While writing the list, did it ever cross your mind to think about your self-care?
- If your answer is "No," Why not?

The above points are a quick assessment of what matters to you the most. Right now, if I ask people to mention the two biggest things they would like to achieve by the end of this year, some will be unsure, while some will have needs like: get a job, buy a house, pay their children's fees and have food. Only a handful of people will say things like, "I want to increase my relaxation time, sleep right, rest well, stress less, and take regular breaks."

You are the most valuable and biggest priority when it comes to goal setting. Nothing takes shape without good health; neither can any of your goals be actualized. You deserve the number one spot in your goal-setting list because that is where you truly belong. It takes someone who is mentally, physically, emotionally, and psychologically stable to undertake and execute goals.

As a game-changer, your overall well-being should be a top priority. Create time to ease stress. Check out this famous quote: "All work and no play make Jack a dull boy." Excessive work dampens the efficiency of the brain and reduces productivity. Be intentional when writing a priority list. Remember, self-care is your lifeline to wealth and success.

Genuine self-care is knowing what you can accomplish now, and later. This knowledge sets the pace for success. It is outright wisdom to know when to take a break, irrespective of how pressing a task is. Don't wait to get to your breaking point before taking a break. Some people break down before their breakthroughs. When you think of ignoring your health, think of what you stand to lose and the troubles that come with it. Do not push yourself beyond limits; be mindful of your health to avoid being burned out before your season of triumph.

Learn to applaud accomplished tasks, give yourself a pat on the back. Say kind and affirming words in a silent whisper or however you feel comfortable to do. Saying it as many times as you wish does not harm so long as it makes you feel good. Words like, "Thank God I did it, I am capable, I am an achiever, congratulations, I made it, I am more than enough, my today is better than my yesterday and my tomorrow will be greater than my today." You can go ahead and make your own affirmations and get into the habit of confessing it daily, twice, or thrice, or as many times as you deem it fit. These words can be very soothing, hopeful, faith-bound, as well as encouraging.

Focus more on the things that bring you joy and peace and the stuff that gives you happiness. If healthy socialization makes you happy, go for it; if it's rest, go ahead and rest. Above all, ensure you incorporate exercise and healthy living into your routine. Success should not be all about the external; it is also important to take care of your inner well-being. You will achieve more with good health. It was John Spencer who said, "Rest is not a luxury you earn when you are finished with creative work. It's a discipline you cultivate to make you more creative."

CHAPTER 6

Test the Waters

> *Twenty years from now you will be more disappointed by the things that you didn't do than by the ones you did do. So throw off the bowlines. Sail away from the safe harbor. Catch the trade winds in your sails. Explore. Dream. Discover.* —Mark Twain

Now that you are through with reading Chapters One to Five, buckle up and get ready for a dive. Be prepared to explore all that is in the water. It will be a total waste of all the work you've done to discover who you are if you fail to step out. Take the risk to find out what is in store for you. In this adventure, two things can happen when you step out: you are either announced or drowned. Step out; if you must fail, it is better to fail early and have the time to pull yourself together. Peradventure, if you did not get it right the first time, cheer up! Try again. It is in failing that we find the determination to do better, if we step out to test the water and succeed, bravo! Repeat the process.

Testing the water gives you a feel of the temperature, whether it is hot or cold. Step out and take risks; show the world what you've got to offer. Are you a speaker? Go out and show the world what you can do. Do you have the skill of coaching? Someone is currently waiting for you. Expose those hidden talents for people to experience. It is time to off-load the knowledge you have gathered to create room for more.

Why wait when the world is waiting for you? Don't be hindered by self-doubt; there are great treasures stored on your inside, launch out. You can't go wrong in the face of tests, but you can learn some lessons for your growth. Shying away from testing the waters is like having a gun and not wanting to pull the trigger. There is no point in learning and knowing so much about yourself when you are unwilling to take a leap.

Life is all about taking risks; from the time we wake up to the time we go to bed; even our sleep time is risky. It is difficult to predict the next event that would likely occur. Taking risks does not only consist of the big stuff, like jumping out of a plane with a parachute or off the cliff, but small things can also be risky.

It is possible to have a job today and be without one the next day. Cooking is a risk; you can accidentally cut your finger while slicing an onion. Driving in a vehicle is equally risky; irrespective of how careful you are, it is difficult to control the outcome of the next driver. We may encounter other forms of risks daily, such as talking to strangers; and even taking a walk. Writing this book was also a risk even when I didn't know if it would sell. Whether you like it or not, risk will always be a significant part of our lives. Stop safeguarding yourself against a fall; let loose.

The gains of stepping out

Success is static; it will never meet you halfway. A considerable amount of effort is required on our path to embrace it. A child who refuses to take a step forward will never know that he can stand; neither will he experience the joy of walking. Some of those early steps come with countless falls, which could be painful enough to deter the child from attempting again. However, if he persists, he will not only learn how to walk but run, jump, climb, dance, and do a lot more. As adults, we need to borrow a cue from children. Stepping out does not exempt us from falling, but no matter how many times we fall, we need to learn to pick ourselves up like a child. If we do, soon, we will grow from standing to walking, from walking to running, and from running to soaring. I hope these progressive processes will inspire you to step out.

Everything in life requires action, whether it is eating, talking, or dancing. Stepping out to take risks can be very intimidating and scary, especially when we are ignorant of what lies ahead. At the same time, it can be extremely rewarding when we carry on without quitting. It reveals some of our hidden potentials. It is in stepping out that you will uncover your unique qualities and the power to overcome your fears like the ones below:

- **Silent fear:** You have the skills to silence that tiny voice that whispers to your heart of how incapable you are.

It comes with the temptation to hold you down and make you resist exploring. Fear is crippled when we take action and venture to try new things. It offers us the atmosphere to boost our self-image and gives us the audacity to fight for a comeback after setbacks. This act ushers us into a realm of no retreat, no surrender. Develop a positive mindset. Remind yourself that difficult times are not forever.

- **Stand out:** It equips you with the strategies on how to become outstanding in all your endeavours. Standing out broadens our circle of influence and showcases us as experts in our domain. At this level, people begin to take note of what we have to offer, which in turn boosts our self-esteem. Your credibility and confidence level are enhanced when you stand out.

- **Creates opportunities:** All risk does not necessarily pay off but refuse to fret if you fail in the process of stepping out. You may be stepping out to explore your skills and on the other hand stumble on new opportunities along the way. Some of these opportunities could result in your growth. It is essential to align yourself with people who can help you identify and create opportunities.

- **Exemplary lifestyle:** This attribute gives you the confidence to function as a role model. It provides you with the opportunity for people to look up to you. Stepping out allows you to frame your overall personality to suit your improved status. It brings about discipline on how to conduct yourself to meet expectations.

Currently, I am cautious of my conduct in public due to my numerous public engagements. I write and post videos to inspire people become pathfinders. I'm also a public speaker, coach, mentor, and some organizations use my books as a teaching guide for their students and staff. This exposure automatically places me in a position of authority and under public scrutiny. Presently, I receive calls, text messages, and emails from people in different parts of the world, letting me know how my videos and social media contents impacted their lives.

- **Life lessons:** "No matter who tries to teach you lessons about life; you won't understand it until you go through it on your own." — Robert Mitchum. Irrespective of the knowledge we acquire, the things we tend to remember the most are the lessons we learn on our own. Lessons learned from stepping out of your comfort zone have a way of staying glued in your memory for years. Reading from a book is not the same as real-life experiences you've had. Real life experiences hand you the firsthand knowledge required to make your life count.

The things I learned in the process of writing this book are far greater than what I read from the internet and what my book coach taught me. I was able to discover many things on my own as soon as I began to write. Those experiences and lessons will forever remain concrete in my heart of hearts. They are one of my most valued assets.

No pain no gain

Taking risk is great, but it comes with pains and gains. The gain associated with it is far greater than not attempting to take any. When you open yourself to one, be prepared to face the challenges that come with it. The ability to predict the end from the beginning might be difficult; even the things you believed that you had a good prediction over can sometimes go wrong. Get ready for unexpected events. Anything can happen when you venture into strange territories with the hopes of succeeding.

Be optimistic wherever you find yourself and in whatever you do. Always hope for the best and look forward to the bright side of life. Some people, before even embarking on any adventure, already visualize the negativity of not going far. They have questions to back up their fears. Questions like what if I fail? What if I lose so much money? What if it does not go well as planned? The only way for them to find out the answers to these questions is to step out. Often, what they are afraid of; may likely manifest because they allowed their fears to becloud their senses.

Some people would want to hold back and play safe rather than explore into an unpredicted territory if it were possible. It is quite intimidating to do what you know may backfire and cause financial hardship if it doesn't go well. Investing a fortune in a risky business can be challenging. Ascending to the top is expensive and is dependent on how much risk you are willing to undertake. Understand your breaking point, and design your risks in such a way that it does not hurt you. It is paramount to know what you can handle at a given time.

Even though stepping out to take risks sometimes comes with gains. However, it has its pains, and some losses could be very heartbreaking when it happens like the ones highlighted below:

- **Trust**: A bridge of trust occurs when terms of agreements are neglected. In some cases, it might not be any fault of yours when things spiral out of your control, and did not happen as planned. People who believed and trusted you might become resentful, which could mar your reputation and credibility. Lack of trust could result in people dissociating from you and this can further reduce your sphere of influence.

- **Criticism**: The naysayers will always be there to challenge your effort in any failed attempts. This situation can sometimes be frustrating to manage, especially if other parties are involved in the failed deal. You may be held responsible for those losses. Criticism is one of the pains that comes with stepping out and could be detrimental to your health.

- **Reduces sphere of influence:** It crashes the number of people who initially believed and looked up to you. People are impatient these days; they might not have the time to stick around for long when the chips are down. They are bound to move on when quality is compromised. This may hamper growth during a re-launch or come-back after a setback. It may take time for people to believe and trust in your brand. A comeback requires significant amount of work; this means having to work ten times harder to regain trust and confidence. This can sometimes result in mental and psychological stress.

- **Kills motivation:** Failure due to stepping out to explore can discourage you from daring again. A failed attempt kills motivation and makes it harder to envision success in the next outing. It weakens the drive and motivation to start all over again. Result drives growth, and when there is none, it kills motivation. The overall wellbeing of a person could be affected because of this.

- **Fear and doubt:** This brings about loss of confidence that makes people question their abilities. Fear of the unknown discourages a person from daring to take risk again and could lead to self-doubt. Those who are faced with this dilemma often view themselves as victims of misfortune and failure.

Regardless of all the pains and setbacks, chose to stay positive, don't give up. Walk with your head held high; you can rewrite your failures if you don't quit. Even extremely planned projects do fail; so, you are not an exception. No one told you the road to greatness would be easy. You just found out by yourself. Despite the hassles, you can still excel. Michael Jordan had this to say: "I can accept failure. Everybody fails at something. But I cannot accept not trying. Fear is an illusion." And so, step out and try to make things happen. You have greatness inside of you.

Withhold nothing — unveil

A flowing river never stinks; neither does it run dry. It is in flowing that its freshness is maintained. When stepping out to take risks, refuse to hold back; give your all and hope for the best. Withholding is like hiding the secrets of success from yourself. Some of the things you are withholding could be the missing puzzle to your success.

Hoarding your skills or knowledge can lead to dryness, which truncates advancement. Knowledge not shared dies with you and can leave you without a successor. If you don't unveil those hidden talents of yours, people are likely to bypass you because they are unaware of your abilities. Those who are scared of sharing ideas end up being redundant. They are afraid that the beneficiary of their knowledge could end up doing better than them. Knowledge not shared is knowledge lost. What you withhold goes extinct and results in a limited lifespan.

Your intellectual ability is far bigger than you and should not be consumed alone. The fact is that your conceived idea of yesterday and even that of today might not be new; someone else must have worked on it. And there is nothing you will do tomorrow that others will not attempt or have not done. The ideas you keep to yourself are short-lived. Someone can unravel the codes to those ideas, the very thing you've been hoarding. It is quite easy to lose a concept and knowledge that is not shared or replicated.

The pen you write with, the chair you sit on, the shoes you wear, the bed you lie on are all products of shared knowledge and skills. Those who came up with those products have impacted numerous lives and are still impacting more. To add to this, some of them are successful due to their shared wealth of knowledge.

The statement below is a reflection of those who hoard and keep what they know to themselves. But when bypassed, say words like:

- Oh, I knew it, but I didn't take action
- I was waiting for the right time
- Wow! Look at how successful that idea is, I wish I did it
- I didn't think it would be a huge success
- I wanted everything to fall in place before taking action
- That is what I wanted to say
- That should have been my idea

Some may be wondering, "Why should I share my idea?" Isn't that supposed to be my trade secret?" I agree; some things are meant to be kept secret. However, trade secrets are supposed to be structured in such a way that would be beneficial to others and yourself. If you are ambivalent about why you need to share your ideas, the questions below will give you a hint on the stuff that can be shared and the ones that should be withheld.

You can start by analyzing the pros and cons and also asking and answering the following questions on "Holding back."

- Do I have any idea, skills, or knowledge to share?
- If yes, what is it?
- Should it be restricted to only me or shared with others?

- Is there any benefit for keeping my ideas and knowledge to myself alone?
- What do I stand to gain if I share it with others?
- Why am I holding back? Is it out of fear or lack of confidence?

If your answers to the questions are yes; it will lead you to the next set of questions:

- How can I leverage on my knowledge and ideas?
- Can my knowledge and idea be monetized?
- Can I raise successors to impact others positively?

All these questions and your answers will help you make the right decision on whether to hold back or share your ideas. However, what you decide to do with your knowledge and ideas are entirely up to you. The important thing is for you to find inner satisfaction and peace with your decision. I have done both; there were moments I felt it was necessary to withhold. It was a phase in my life. There are also phases that I decided to offer my knowledge for free. As I continue to step out of my comfort zones, I realize that my intellectual abilities could be monetized rather than give it all up for free. This led to the development of my program, Pathfinders Masters, where I coach and support individuals to achieve their goals. By choosing to share my knowledge, I am impacting lives while earning income at the same time. I believe that with all the above strategies, my ideas and expertise will outlive me as I continue to serve others.

You stand to lose nothing by unveiling your talents and ideas for people to feast on. Unfortunately, most people only give a little or a piece of themselves, hoping that it will get them further in life. In most cases, people who refuse to pass on their expertise tend to forget the knowledge they do not share.

In my early days of writing, I had the impression that holding back content would hand me more content to carry on with my writing for a while. But I soon realized that the more I held back, the more difficult it was for me to craft more words. If I did not release myself to flow freely, several chapters like this one, Testing the Waters, would not have appeared in this book because my intention was to reserve it for another book. But as soon as I made up my mind to allow the contents flow, I was amazed at how much words I had inside of me to pour out. I started with writing one book but ended up writing two books. As it stands right now, I don't have to worry about the contents for my third and fourth books because these days, the words flow freely whenever I hop on the keyboard to type. With this guiding principle, I am on a mission to writing many more books. Your riches and success are all within you.

CHAPTER 7

Expect the Unexpected

There are times we expect things to happen in a particular way and pattern, but it ends up happening in the exact opposite direction and flaws our expectation. Maybe you started a business and hoped it would flourish, only for the business to take a nosedive in the wrong direction. Some started a job they didn't think would be a perfect match, and then it turned out to be their ideal job. There is always a twist to life, so be prepared for the long haul and be ready to flow as it unravels. Expected and unexpected events are an inevitable part of our lives and cannot be bypassed.

When you think of the word "unexpected," what comes to your mind? Is it all about sad events? Some believe the phrase "unexpected" is synonymous to tragic occurrences, like the loss of loved ones or sicknesses. No! Good things also happen unexpectedly, like having a surprise birthday party, or a surprise car gift. Surprises in this context are healthy. Some surprises come with anguish and try to steal our peace and joy. However, in this chapter, we are addressing the unforeseen events that affect our mental state.

An Unexpected event is no respecter of persons; it can happen to anyone, both young and old. For instance, a child who has mastered the art of playing piano excellently well; steps up to the podium to play, and then, the unpredictable happens. He suddenly forgets how to strike the notes on the keyboard due to stage fright. A similar experience could also happen to an adult who started a business and believed it would be remarkably successful only to discover that it was situated in a wrong location, leading to its collapse. Anything can happen in life.

People get worked up when things spiral out of their control; they yell, scream, punch the wall, regret, blame, kick the air, and feel depressed. In your case, what would you do if things did not work out according to plan?

Chapter Six of this book - Test the Waters, talks about how things could go wrong when we decide to step out and explore. It is not wrong for things to go against your expectation, but how you react in that moment could worsen or brighten the situation. Here are a few things to consider in the face of unexpected circumstances:

Think twice

Most people react to things rather than respond. They might choose to walk away from the scene when situations negate their expectation, irrespective of the consequences. Taking a break to think twice could be helpful; it gives you the opportunity to figure out what to do. Instant reactions to unpleasant occurrences could end in a lifetime of regret.

The setbacks that came with delving into the business world were enormous for me. There were some swift actions that I took when I got entangled in a desperate situation. After receiving business training under my mother's watch in Nigeria, I was sure of soaring high wherever I found myself. She was a petty trader in foodstuff, and I loved accompanying her to the market. In the process, I got exposed to most of the skills that I possess today. My customer service skills, attention to detail, effective communication, time management, interpersonal skills, and many others grew extensively under her guidance.

My strong inclination to business manifested at an early stage of my life. After working a few years in Africa, Middle East, and North America, I decided to take a bow from the corporate industry to pursue my passion in the business world.

Two years after my arrival in Canada, I took a step towards starting a business in childcare. After spending my childhood and part of my adult life in business, I was optimistic that it would succeed. To my utmost surprise, it did not turn out the way I envisioned. All my expectations came crashing. My initial reaction was to quit, but instead, I paused, and analyzed the whole process. It dawned on me that I did not spend enough time to learn how to develop sustainable systems and structures. These were the essential requirements that I needed for the successful growth of my childcare business.

These challenges awakened my curiosity to a point that, I had to take a step back to reflect on the circumstances which led to my failure. Those moments of reflection turned things around. As I revisited the processes, I was able to identify my flaws and I laid out sustainable plans to correct the errors. These experiences aroused a hunger in me for success.

Be tactical

Life is all about strategy, be prepared to embrace changes as you sail through unexpected situations. Even when we plan for the best, things can go in the opposite direction. Don't be dismayed when confronted with the worst conditions. Keep your dreams alive by clinging tight to the big picture; the best will inevitably show up. Hold on.

Being tactical can help proffer solutions to stressful events. Device strategies that can help you recreate your world, and carefully implement them. It will give you a winning edge on how to overcome difficult seasons.

My initial struggle with the childcare business helped broadened my perspective and gave me the guidance needed to run a successful business. As I progressed, I asked a series of questions and got answers. Those answers provided me with the clarity to forge ahead. Here are some of the questions:

- What are systems and structures?
- Does my business need one?
- How do I set up one?
- Where do I start?
- Where can I find support?
- What are the benefits of systems and structures?
- Will it be sustainable?
- What if it doesn't work?

After answering the questions, I set out to work. I mapped out different strategies to help me flip my struggles into success and it worked to my advantage.

Start again

Encountering roadblocks is not enough reason to make a U-turn or surrender. We all have a part to play in the quest for success. You may have gone through severe challenges that may have impeded your drive for starting all over again; however, you can still excel irrespective of your failures. Make up your mind to stay determined and committed. Stressing over negativities could weary and disorient the mind. I believe reading this paragraph will challenge you to think deeply as well as equip you with the right tactics to plan for your breakthrough.

Experiencing hiccups on your way to success should not make you abandon or take a bow from your projects. When you are stuck, activate your creative thought pattern, and come up with an alternate route to arrive at your destination. Starting all over does not mean remaining in stuff that is bound to fail. It is in the process that you get to discover your abilities and inabilities. People have missed great opportunities because they chose to walk away when the going was tough.

A person who failed at becoming a pilot or a lawyer will remain perpetually down if he refuses to try again or do something new. The same goes for a child who refuses to walk because he fell and hurt himself while learning how to walk; that child will never experience the joy of walking, running, or even jumping. Anyone can grow fast if they are committed to the end.

Beginning all over from the scratch may not imply outright success but agreeing to start again marks the beginning of your winning. It does not matter if you fail; what matters the most is your willingness to try again. Failing gives you the fortitude to keep trying, and one day, you will become a champion with those challenging experiences. Not wanting to start again because of setbacks is worse than failure itself.

My failed experiences with the childcare centre nearly resulted in abandoning the business. I was ready to let go of all my investment, the sacrifices, labour, and my effort in starting the business. With all the difficulties that stared at me, I didn't think I would survive those hard times. Doubt and fear almost crippled me from restarting, but I have come to understand they are not the villains. Despite all the struggles and failures, I summoned the bravery to start again; I was determined to arrive at my end goal.

Do not despise

Some people worry about starting small especially in situations where they have to restart from the scratch, after a failed attempt. This experience can be psychologically demanding. Starting small is not a sign of weakness but staying small should be discouraged. If you dread going through the process again or decide to remain small after a failed venture, you might have a glimpse of your end goal but unable to reach it.

My desire was and has always been to work for big organizations, but after applying for countless jobs without scaling through, I opted to work for a small organization against my expectation. The salary was only a token. However, I embraced my role wholeheartedly and gave my best without holding back. I got exposed to challenging tasks, most of which were beyond my competence. I remembered saying "No" to most of the jobs that came my way because I was too afraid to fail at them; besides, serving from behind-the-scenes was my flair.

Before now, being led by others felt excellent and perfect because I didn't think I possessed the quality to lead. Yet, here I was being tasked with tremendous responsibilities that included but were not limited to leading teams: writing, coordinating meetings, public speaking, representing the organization in conferences, developing systems and processes, managing others, making decisions, and training both new and old staff. The list was endless.

My words, "No, I can't," eventually turned into "Yes, I can." This handed me the audacity to do the unimaginable, and surprisingly, I excelled at them. My fear and phobia for working for a small organization flipped to my advantage. The very things I despised and considered as minor at the beginning became instrumental to my advancement and, above all, made me a pathfinder. Keep an open mind; unexpected events do happen, but if you wage a fight against quitting, it will enthrone you in the end.

Broken in pain

Be ready to suck it all up and view pain as part of growth. Most people give up in the face of suffering and brokenness after they have failed. The phrase "No Pain, No Gain," is to develop resilience in the face of adversities. Let the picture of your end goal give you the strength to endure hardship. When you are held bound by pain to the point of wanting to take a bow, look inward, and think about the joy of success and the very reason you started. That joy will give you the antidote to numb those pains. Be tenacious because there is no easy way out to success.

Before starting the childcare centre, I expected to see it blossom, and turn out great even though it was situated in a low-income community. My goal was to provide a quality childcare service in the community to impact lives. On this note, I decided to set up an environment that reflected a home away from home for children, where they would feel free, safe, and loved to learn and explore.

The centre began in full swing with my four children as the first registered pupil. I worked tirelessly to bring in clients, and in the third month, students began to trickle in, and the number continued to increase with each passing month. The growth was impressive, and my joy knew no bounds. As time went by, I discovered that some parents needed additional support apart from serving their children. They were in search of someone they could share their daily struggles with. It was apparent; they wanted more than just a childcare service. They needed some form of encouragement to enable them sail through the pressures of life. Their needs were a perfect blend of my past role in the corporate world. I gladly took up the responsibility to support them to the best of my abilities.

Not long, our hard work filtered into the community, which increased our clientele. Just when I was beginning to gain traction to soar high, the unexpected happened. The centre was recommended to shut down for a major maintenance in the facility. It was heartbreaking to watch all our hard work and effort crash before our eyes in one day. Sadly, we had to vacate everyone, both children and staff for the maintenance to commence.

I wept bitterly about the incident as I watched everyone vacate the centre; it broke me to my bones. I was inconsolable, but my husband and children did all they could to keep me calm. They gave me hope against hopelessness with their soothing words. This pain brought about my longing to write amid brokenness. In that state, I was able to unveil this book, Be Your Pathfinder. Writing this book at the time I did, brought so much healing to me. I drew courage from the pages as I poured out my heart in writing. Some pages were emotional and brought tears to my eyes, while some calmed my nerves and gave me the strength to forge ahead. My brokenness left me with evidence and a voice for the world in the pages of this book.

The centre was re-opened after three months of closure, and we had to start all over again. Although starting from scratch was extremely challenging, but we had to. It took so much hard work to get to where we were before the closure. However, we began to build the business again, and just when I thought the coast was clear for a smooth ride, I was faced again with another challenge. Most parents could not afford to pay their children's fees due to job loss and personal problems. Siting a business in a low-income community comes with its unique struggles. However, it is worth all the sacrifices.

Even though I was financially handicapped at that time, I lacked the courage to turn back those children due to unpaid fees. Looking at their innocent eyes, I had to write off their fees. I am yet to turn any child away because of outstanding fees, and I don't intend doing so. As crazy as this may sound, I chose to use it as a token of my contribution to humanity, it is one of my unique ways of giving back to the community. I believe life does not consist of money alone but acts of kindness. Sometimes, you lose, and sometimes you gain.

Success is sacrificial; it is costly. There must be a noticeable physical change for a woman to carry a baby in her womb for nine months. She will have to undergo so much discomfort, nausea, vomiting, and having to sleep on her sides for the duration of the pregnancy. Not to mention labour and delivery, this could sometimes result in complications. But as soon as the baby is born, the pain becomes history. She forgets about all the discomfort and celebrates the joy of having a baby more than she remembers the pain. Sometimes, pain is a track record of success. And so, it was with my childcare business; I believe that someday, I will look back with a heart full of thanksgiving for all my labour of love.

Regrets

Very often, we are filled with regrets when the unexpected happens. Life has a way of making us feel trapped and defeated when things don't go right. It makes us to wish that we never stepped out and blame ourselves and maybe others for the problems. This places us in a self-nagging state.

Regret is not bad in totality; it is okay to regret our bad decisions or inappropriate actions that we engage in. Regret, if neglected, could dampen our spirit. Every experience comes with its unique lesson; learn a lesson or two to keep you on course. I have had my fair share of regret due to my poor decisions. I am learning as much as possible to manage a life of regret over any attempts I have embarked on in my journey to greatness.

The joy of starting the centre and the pain of closure will never elude me. I still remember those moments of regretting and wishing I never started the business. But I have moved past that phase. Those moments of disappointment, tears, and torture are all tools that have changed the trajectory of my setbacks. It gave me the stamina to be fearless in the face of pressures. I have grown from that experience and the childcare centre has also grown tremendously.

Living continually in regret is like facing backward to walk down your path. This can prevent you from seeing what is coming while maintaining focus on what has already happened. Live a life full of gratitude, regardless of your experiences. Some disappointments are necessary to propel you in the right path. Choose to live above it.

Shift to excel

Embarking on any significant shifts is risky and can be both exciting and fearful. Whether starting a marital life, new business, immigrating to a new country, starting school, or changing careers, these shifts often come with mixed feelings. You may be conversant with the beginning but knowing the end might evade you.

As I take on more business vicinities, I am confident that no obstacle can stop me. I have developed a thick skin against impending obstacles with the knowledge I have acquired. When I took the risk of starting the childcare centre, I never imagined that it would be successful.

Presently, what began as a seed of an acorn has gradually evolved into an oak tree. The centre is fast spreading its tentacles with two locations in the province of Alberta, Canada. It wasn't a comfortable journey, but it is worth it. I am thankful to God that we made it through despite the numerous challenges.

Be rooted in whatever you do. Some unexpected experiences have the power to shift you into greatness. Apart from the expansion of the centre, it has unveiled diverse new ways for me to continually impact lives. This experience has made me a mentor and coach to upcoming authors, teachers, entrepreneurs, students, women, and more. I have come to understand that imperfection or unexpected change in direction does not connote failure; but could end in big wins.

CHAPTER 8

Just Breathe

Reading through the pages of this book might be quite daunting for some people. They may be distracted by other pressing issues. Often, you hear some people say, "I'm a very busy person." Some others would say stuff like, "I find it difficult to sit still without engaging in one activity or the other." Some even get busy to the point that; they create activities to keep them on their feet most of the time. I used to be that mom who would roam around the house, looking for an additional task to add to my existing ones. I would push beyond my limits. This attitude, even though it yielded the result of a clean environment, did not turnout great. It often caused setbacks in other areas of my life.

Being busy is not an issue, but the execution process is paramount. If you are working for someone, trust and integrity could be affected if the job is not proficiently implemented. Taking on several responsibilities, beyond your capabilities could result in internal and external risks. This can show up as a weakness and could negatively impact your mental, emotional, and psychological state. We are not superhumans, and as such, we need to come to a place where we can exhale after working hard.

Every athlete comes to that point of exhaustion where all they need is to just breathe. The pressures of life often lead us to this point. When we accept numerous tasks, we are likely to end up in a stressful state which could obstruct our overall wellbeing.

Our bodies have a way of giving us signals when it is under stress. Those signs can appear in diverse ways to alert us of the danger ahead. Symptoms like tiredness, yawning, blurry vision, head and body aches, dizziness, and maybe driving and napping while trying hard to stay awake might show up. Nobody knows your body more than you do; the onus lies on you to know when to call it a day. You don't have to pay someone to tell you when to take a break. You owe yourself that responsibility, rise up and do it for yourself.

Some people attempt to impress others; maybe their bosses, friends, family members, or even themselves, and as such, they take on numerous tasks that stress them out. This could result in poor health condition. Depending on its severity, one might not be strong enough or live to tell the story. Be smart to shake off extreme fatigue off your radar.

The jobs, calls, text messages, and invitations will always be there; you don't have to respond to all of it. You are only one person with twenty-four hours a day. You can't do everything and be everywhere at the same time. Running around from one point to another does not make you an achiever; instead, you may end up with an extremely confused mindset and exhaustion. Learn to decline excessive commitments, pause, and prioritize in order of preference when necessary.

Intentionally create time to relax. It will enable you to function efficiently. Now, and again we get entangled with stressful work habits that impede our time of relaxation. The burdens of life can easily distract us from resting. The ability to calmly deal with life's issues is particularly important to maintain a progressive and healthy lifestyle.

Creating an enabling environment to relax is crucial. Taking breaks does not necessarily mean taking the whole day to rest. Just having two to ten minutes of walking away from strenuous tasks can be quite refreshing. When you've made up your mind to rest, try as much as possible to detach yourself from thoughts that cause your mind to wander. Some of these worries, if overlooked, could lead to unnecessary anxiety. As humans with excessive mental activities, it is difficult to shut down completely. But being intentional with your time of breaks can help minimize distractions and fatigue.

Some people get deeply rooted in meeting deadlines to the extent that they forget to take breaks. In many cases, taking time to rest takes the back seat, especially when there are pending issues to be addressed. No matter how pressing the task at hand is, one has to be willful with rest. Invest in the stuff that helps you relax, whether exercising, dancing, reading, lying down, or watching a movie. Try as much as possible to switch off completely to give your body permission to embrace its state of rest.

Order of preference

When drawing up a schedule, it is vital to accommodate breaks and make it a priority. Your mind is likely to roam about when you don't have a list of preference to keep it in check. Creating a to-do list can help streamline inefficiency and unnecessary waste of time. Be sensitive to know when to shuffle things around. Create room for flexibility. The ability to work with an order of preference is critical to managing time effectively.

Abraham Lincoln once said, "Give me six hours to chop down a tree and I will spend the first four sharpening the axe." Knowing your first line of action in any situation will help you go far as well as eliminates distraction. Avoid heaping piles of work that you have no insight into the work involved and the time required to getting it done. Very often, when you discover how enormous a workload is, it might become unexciting and wearisome to do. Some people are in the habit of piling jobs they have not assessed and are clueless of the gravity of work involved.

People have lost out on great opportunities not because they are bad at what they do, but because the volume of tasks they got entrapped with was overwhelming, which made them appear inefficient. It is better to space out tasks so that you can have the opportunity to produce excellent pieces of work. Poor job delivery can mar your reputation; don't take things for granted; be committed to setting up a list of preferences before working on any tasks.

Be hopeful and believe that everything will be alright despite the pressures around you, learn to take one step at a time. As you go about executing your tasks, remember there is always another day to resolve any unresolved issues. Working with a mindset of proffering solutions to every problem could result in fatigue. There is only so much you can do in a certain amount of time. There comes a time when you have to slow down; just breathe, exhale, and relax.

Another day

There is nothing much you can do with a limited amount of time. Even though the twenty-four hours embedded in a day increases to fifty-four, it will still be insufficient for most people. There will always be pressing needs to swallow up that time. It is essential to know how to work around your time to stay productive. Strategically apportion time to accommodate vital activities such as work, rest, family time, social life, shopping, spousal, children, and study time. The ability to make them fit perfectly well in the twenty-four hours requires a lot of effort and discipline because time is never enough.

Live life knowing that there is tomorrow; taking one extra day to get work done thoroughly does not connote setbacks. It is common sense to know when to stop pushing beyond your limits. Take breaks when necessary. The pressures of getting tasks done at a specific time and day could render us incapable of functioning effectively the next day. You may wake up the next day feeling very exhausted to carry on with other pending tasks in the right frame of mind.

As the saying goes, "Rome was not built in a day." There is no need to burn out before reaching your goals. Accept setbacks as part of progress, view it as a time to rest, and be willing to adjust when there is a need to do so.

In writing this book, I faced many awkward moments that required me to rest. Some days were extremely hectic due to heavy workloads. At such times, I gave in to naps, sleep, and indulged in the stuff that made me happy to replenish my lost energy. I would even skip writing for days just to get refreshed based on my mental and physical state. Did all this affect my timeline? "Yes, of course it did." But I cared less because those breaks were much needed. It gave me the time to rejuvenate my mind, soul, and body for efficiency.

I have learned from experience that hard work pays, but working smart pays even more. I have also learned to be attentive to my breaking points, having in mind that I am in competition with no one other than myself. This mindset has gotten me into the habit of approaching issues one day at a time. I have come to understand that what I cannot complete today can be completed tomorrow. There is always another day; be purposeful about your aspirations and the big picture.

Give others a chance

As a pathfinder, it is important to give others a chance. Having people around and not effectively engaging them is a sheer waste of human resources. Agreeing to do everything alone can lead to frustration and stress. Make a to-do list of what others can do and what you are best at doing. Delegate the things you are aware others can handle to create time for your core areas of expertise. This approach yields high level of efficiency and maximum productivity.

The body, most notably the brain, is not designed to function as a working machine. You cannot do everything alone, create an outlet for people to carry out their jobs with minimal interference. Trust and give them the freedom to make mistakes, learn, and grow in their assigned tasks. Life is not all about you and will never be, you will give people a chance when you understand this principle. You will continually be in denial of people's capabilities and limitations until you give them the opportunity to try. Stop clinging onto everything, withdraw from disproportionate engagements. Trust people to be able to complete tasks in their unique ways. Let your focus be on the big picture.

When I began trusting and giving people the power to carry out their assigned jobs uninterruptedly, it opened more doors for me to accomplish more goals. Be considerate of your health; permit people to help where necessary. Being strategic can result in the effective and efficient utilization of human resources.

The danger of fear

Fear makes people do things they would not dare to do, and vice versa. Fear of being mocked if things don't go as planned has wreaked havoc on people's health. The fear of unforeseen circumstances can cause one to work without taking a break. Below are some of the reasons people sacrifice their time to work at the expense of their health:

- Fear of failure
- I want to prove a point
- What will people say?
- I don't want to be a loser
- If I don't do it now, someone else will take my place
- I will be mocked
- I might be broke
- I may never have the opportunity again

Most people work themselves to a state of mental instability due to fear. Oftentimes, we fail to remember that we need sound health and mind to execute sound judgments. Even though fear is a vital part of our existence, make a conscious effort to keep it under control because there will always be things that will negate our plans. If all the worries have not been able to change anything in your life, then why worry over what you cannot change? Keep your focus on what you have the power to control. Just breathe and let go of what you cannot control.

Although fear is detrimental to our health, however, it has its unique side. The same fear that destroys can also build. The fear that makes you fail can bring you success. It made me work much harder to ensure that failure met with success in my childcare business. The fear of, "What if I fail, and what will people say?" almost ruined my dreams and aspirations.

Most times, we create unnecessary pressure around ourselves that often end up attacking us. When you come to terms with all the havoc, fear has caused; it will arouse a desire in you to wage war against it. Instead of feeding your mind with thoughts of how you will likely fail, reinstate your notion with positivity and declare, "I will succeed." Swing those "what if I fail?" to "what if I succeed?" Everything is possible; all you have to do is to believe and take the right steps towards your goals. It will all end in your advantage. Just breathe.

Success redefined

You are your own success, what you do with yourself today will determine what tomorrow will bring and how you will end up. People define success according to their perception, wants, and needs. Some say real success is in serving others. Yes, helping others is excellent, but more importantly, you need to master the act of serving yourself first before you can think of serving others. Doing that places you in a position to help others more adequately. You cannot be in a bad shape and be able to render services. I hear this phrase a lot: "You cannot give what you don't have." It is challenging to embrace success when you think or view life as a bed of roses, without giving room for the various seasons in between. Success comes in different shades. People define it in distinctive ways, and according to their preference. Some believe that true success is in:

Material wealth: Having material possession is excellent; pause and think about this; what importance is material wealth if it does not add value to others?

Giving to others: Giving is exceptional. But remember we all have needs. Be humble enough to receive from others when possible, even if it›s just a smile or compliments, it only makes you human because nobody is without want. When someone tells you that, "Your ring is beautiful." Smile and say, "Thank you," instead of trying to explain how long you have had it for.

Health and self-care: Health and self-care are phenomenal ways to succeed. Being fit enables you to create more impact and strengthen you to be of service to others. Your health is your lifeline to success.

Receiving from others: Being a receiver does not harm, but take a step back, look inward, and ask yourself this question, what can I offer to others in return? Everyone has something to offer, regardless of how little.

There is no right or wrong definition to success; it appeals to people differently, and Irrespective of the category you belong to, understand that success without impact is meaningless.

    I had no idea how difficult it was for me to receive until I was involved in a terrible accident and needed assistance to sit up, dress, cook, and do more. Often, I would drag myself out of bed in pain to serve myself despite the plea from loved ones to take a break. It felt awkward to accept such level of care because I wasn't conversant to receiving in that capacity. Like me, some people find it easier to care for others than to receive care. We need to break free from this ideology. Be sensitive enough to know when to receive and ask for help.

The narrow escape

May 30th, 2018 will remain evergreen in my memory. A day the unimaginable happened. My centre was still at its infancy stage. As a new business owner, I lacked the required number of clients and staff to run the day-to-day operation. I had invested nearly all my savings and even opted to borrow from financial institutions to support the initial start-up. The bank denied my request because I wasn't qualified, and this mounted a lot of stress on me. As my last option, I resorted to wearing different hats for the business to survive. I became a cleaner by night, driver by day, administrator, recruiter, marketer, accountant, director, and teacher, in addition to my other numerous roles as a mother, wife, and community volunteer, you name it.

I worked tirelessly around the clock, which affected my mental and psychological state, and it completely altered my lifestyle. The fear of failing held me captive; there were days it was difficult for me to sleep due to the financial outlook of the business. Some nights were very rough and made me cry. Allowing the tears to roll down my cheeks freely gave me the coping mechanism to overcome those fearful and terrifying days. Tears have a way of easing stressful times. Shedding a few drops did not imply fragility on my part; rather, it helped me develop the healing balm to cope during those hard moments in the business.

A few months into the business, I was already mentally drained, exhausted, extremely fatigued, and emotionally unstable. Even though it was very glaring, but sometimes, our body has a way of making us believe we can push through that extra task. On one of such days, I was driving home with my five-year-old son after a very hectic day at work. Even though I was extremely fatigued and stressed, I still felt I could handle an extra step as usual. But this time around, I was in total denial, and the unexpected happened.

As I drove home from work that day, suddenly, I heard a thunderous sound - BANG! A collision! It happened so fast at an intersection of a road. I saw my car spinning with its parts scattered in the air in a blurry but vivid vision. When the vehicle finally gained stability, the driver's door where I sat was yanked open. I was dragged out and gently laid by the roadside. The shock from the accident instantly hiked my temperature, which made me shiver. A blanket was flung over me to calm my shivering nerves as I laid numb by the roadside.

I managed to open my eyes just in time to see my five-year-old son being carried away by a total stranger. I wasn't sure if he was okay, he had tears rolling down his cheeks, and his hands stretched toward me as if to say, "Please don't take me away! I need mom!" Those words ignited the strength in me, and I summoned the courage to ask if he was okay. Although I appeared unconscious from the shock, I felt I was very much aware of my environment. It was humbling to be surrounded by well-wishers, paramedics, police officers, and firefighters, all of them doing their bit to ensure that I was okay.

After a while, I began to feel severe aches and body pains; my legs and arms were greatly affected; they were extremely sore and swollen with pains. My back, neck, and joints were not spared; they equally ached in pain. I was transported to the hospital in an ambulance after I was stabilized. I woke up in tears in the hospital to find my husband and five-year-old son who was with me during the accident by my bedside. Even though he was still in tears, thankfully, he was in a good condition.

I struggled to keep calm as the pain intensified with every tick of the clock. I groaned and pleaded with the medical team to have me checked due to the excruciating pain.

Eventually, I went through a series of tests, checks, and X-rays. The results came out better than I anticipated. It was a huge relief to know that I was externally and internally okay except for a minor wrist fracture. I knew God's loving mercy spared my life. It was a major accident; it claimed the vehicle in totality but left my son and me, whole. Through it all, I came out with only a minimal injury.

Although the vehicle was completely lost, however, we walked away with our lives intact. In all of these, I often wonder, "What is a car compared to human lives?" This experience is a constant reminder of how uncertain life can be. It is difficult to predict what the next minute will bring. The intensity of my stress level almost consumed me. Miraculously, I was discharged and sent home for minor physiotherapy on my wrist. Today, I am alive to tell my story of victory. God did it all, and I am exceptionally and eternally grateful.

It was another lesson of a lifetime; I discovered that taking breaks is an integral piece of human existence through my experience with pains and losses. Working without limits can worsen and jeopardize our health. The pressures of life held me hostage so much that I saw taking breaks as a luxury rather than a necessity.

Everyone gets to a breaking point where all they need is just breathe and exhale. No matter who you are, you must come to the point of breathing and exhaling to gain your momentum back. Breathing is living and refreshing to the body and soul. Take a step back and analyze your work ethic; develop strategies and systems to make life easy for you.

The fear of failure mounted unnecessary pressure on me; it stole nearly everything from me. It took away my peace, joy, sleep, car, health, and almost ruined the very business I was fighting hard to save. It did not end there; it nearly snatched my son's life and mine. I have come to realize that uncontrolled fear, and stress could be extremely disastrous. I am eternally grateful that my fears did not consume me; instead, it taught me a lesson and gave me a story to share.

CHAPTER 9

Five R's to Success

> *Successful people begin where failures leave off. Never settle for 'just getting the job done.' Excel!* —Tom Hopkins

Have you ever wondered what the real meaning of success is? As you already saw in Chapter Eight, everyone has a different definition of it. To some, it could be, "If only I can have a spouse or children," or "If only I can have a job or buy a house?" The list continues. What does success mean to you? Everyone has something they are aiming to achieve. Regardless of what you are aiming at, there is a price associated with it. Success does not just fall from the sky; it is guided by principles, and some have obtained theirs with their unique formula.

How would you term a financially stable person who does so much for his community, maybe donates food, sponsors the less privileged through school, and creates job opportunities but has some health challenges? Or what about the guy who is healthy and engages in lots of physical activities to keep fit and train others voluntarily and yet does not have a job? Would you say they are either successful or unsuccessful? Do you prefer one over the other? From the different scenarios, it will be quite complicated to give a straightforward answer.

Some of us base our definition of success on people's appearances: their dressing style, the car they drive, their jobs, houses, the people they associate with, and maybe who they marry. But this might not be an accurate representation of accomplishment. Judging success by physical appearances can be deceptive. It is complicated to make a definite statement on when to say a person is successful or not.

Some people might not have it all. They may only have the necessities of life and good health. Does that mean they are successful or not? It is still difficult to say, right? What, then, is success to you? One can be successful in one area of their life and deficient in another. Despite the hard work the person puts in, there is always that one piece and missing link that needs fixing. No one has it all.

Society views success differently. The fact is, whether we can clearly define success or not, everyone wants to be successful at something; it could be in business, career, personal life, or education. There is always something in our life that we aspire to accomplish. Pick an area you want to succeed at and give it a shot; after that, carry out an assessment to define success in your own personal and unique way.

When doing all of this, remember, success is static; it can never meet you midway. It only embraces you when you have gone all out for it. When you meet with success, it will surely announce you to your world. Like Frank Ocean rightly said, "Work hard in silence; let success be your noise." Actualizing your goals will be farfetched if the big picture is not tangible enough to drive you through the path to meet with it.

Our desire to excel keeps evolving with time. We are insatiable; most of our achievements are short-lived with a passion for more. We are always in search of more attainment to add under our belt. There will always be a new goal to work on; hence, we are continually searching for new accomplishments.

When I reached the goal of starting my childcare centre, I was driven with another goal of bringing in clients in no time. As soon as I accomplished that, another goal sprung up: I wanted to start another childcare centre. And then, writing this book came up, and now, a new goal of getting this book into the readers' hands. The quest for success is endless; it goes on and on. There is always something for us to aspire to do or become. As we keep breaking new grounds and encroaching into new territories, we sometimes forget to celebrate some of our milestones and breakthroughs. Very often, we tend to see our achievements as normal. It is imperative to celebrate all your attainments in any way possible; every hard work deserves to be applauded.

Keep your internal drive and motivation alive by celebrating all your effort to boost more success. Consistently map out a blueprint to guide you. Look for those who have left footprints on the path of greatness and learn from them. Keep building on goals that you have achieved, as well as create new ones. Let these five principles lead you along the path to success:

- Remember
- Reflect
- Refill
- Re-fire
- Re-strategize

The Five R's of success will help you arrive at your end goal. Attaining excellence might be easy but making it sustainable is where most people struggle with. The Five R's principles will prepare you to handle and retain your achievements in every facet of life.

Remember

Some of the things we remember about our lives have brought us to where we are and will inspire us to fight to keep our dreams alive. The memory we have over certain things holds us accountable and to stay focus. When you remember that you must take care of yourself and provide for your family, you will have no choice but to go out and get a job. When you know that people are looking up to you, you will put your act together to function productively in your role.

Some people get stuck halfway and give up because they forget why they started in the first instance. Failing to remember the reason for wanting to succeed, might hamper you from reaching your goal line. There is always a reason for doing or wanting to do anything. Why do you crave for success? Let the answer to that question be your constant reminder and a push to work hard. When the effect of success and failure is in view, it will challenge you to make the right decision for your growth.

As an immigrant, when I think of the reason I travelled out of my country, I have no choice other than to make my life count. I give my best to any job that crosses my way. That means I must go above and beyond the periphery in any assigned task. Some travelled out of the shores of their country for the purpose of schooling, in search of greener pastures, or by virtue of marriage. Whatever reason is responsible for you to have decided to travel out; try as much as possible to make it remarkable.

Setting and achieving goals were a significant part of me before coming to Canada. However, this skill dwindled when I left the shores of my country. I became passive over things, and it took me time to pick back that part of me and to be able to step back into my shoes of goal setting. When I went past that limitation, my mission to actualize my dreams began in earnest; I have achieved a few, however, there are still more to be achieved.

I have heard stories from immigrants who were very influential in their home country before travelling out. They forfeited their luxury, sold their property, and abandoned their professions to make travelling out of their home country a dream come true. But as soon as they depart from their country, they tend to forget all the sacrifices and commitments they undertook to succeed. These people begin to live a life of mere survival and accept defeats as it surfaces. When you forget too soon how successful you were in the past and the sacrifices you paid to make it a reality, you will end up having a seat with failure. Let the memory of your past success energize and inspire you to tread the road of triumph.

Reflect

This is the second principle of success. It is important to take out time to reflect, irrespective of how busy you are. This allows you to look beyond your external to commune with your inner self. Reflecting is like standing in front of a mirror where you can see the scars and stains in order to make the necessary adjustment. Most people are responsive to their external appearances than they are with their inner selves. We find it easy to spend a chunk amount of time in front of a mirror to ensure our physical appearance conforms to our outward image. However, we struggle to align our inner self to stay in tune with growth. The journey to self-reflection begins with remembering who you are and what you want out of life.

Reflection equips you with the opportunity to ask and answer some soul-searching questions on your strengths, weaknesses, and values to become more aware of yourself. It brings to light your abilities and enables you to make the right decisions and to gain clarity.

When you reflect on your inner strength, it paints a mental picture of where you are, where you want to be, and how you can get there. This exposes you to an in-depth insight required for your attainment. When you reflect, it broadens the knowledge of your real value to enable you create the future of your dream and exposes your hidden potentials.

It in reflecting that your mind gets to register new idea for a productive lifestyle. When this occurs, document them for future reference. Those ideas are like a compass that guides you in decision making. This could result in a change in lifestyles, like letting go of self-inflicted pressures. When you reflect, you are empowered to mend your fears and insecurities.

You don't have to experience success or failure before reflecting. This principle enables you to evaluate your performance and to know whether you are making progress or not. It informs you of habits that should be corrected and the ones to be esteemed.

Refill

A refillable container may look empty but has a purpose to serve. The function of the container makes its usage meaningful. Reflecting initiates room for refilling and letting go of what is not needful. Refilling expels the toxic habits and replaces it with healthy and productive ones. After a thorough reflection, I have seen people who refill an already stressful activity with a more stressful and toxic one. Some in an attempt to generate additional income got a new job that is extremely stressful than the previous.

Apply caution when making a choice. Some things are worth considering when making changes, especially if it is in line with a career switch. Your age, physical, mental state, and passion should be taken into consideration.

Imagine a person who is already in her fifties, wanting to venture into a career where lifting is a core component of her job. How sustainable do you think that job will be?

In ten years, when she is in her sixties, her physical strength will pose a huge challenge. At this time, her bones will be weak, and no matter how passionate she is, the strength to carry on will be reduced.

Passion without physical enablement does last long. When this happens, it mars self-esteem; causes one to struggle and could result in stagnation. Before switching careers, find out if what you are about to do is in line with your age and physical abilities to avoid early disengagement. Engaging with the right choice of career brings satisfaction and fulfillment.

Re-fire

There is no point spending time to refill yourself with any profession or studies like nursing, teaching, or public speaking if you have no desire to function in the role. When you spend time and energy to educate yourself, it is expected to explore what you have learned even if it's for leisure. The knowledge that is not used will be trashed. Engaging in what you have learned can inspire others.

Some are experts at engaging and disengaging. It is okay to do things just for fun but occasionally take out some time to experiment on what you have learned. Often, people pay a fortune to learn how to sing and, in the end, never hummed a song for one day? Sometimes, we learn for leisure purposes but try as much as possible to use the knowledge unless they are irrelevant. Think of someone who signed up for piano lessons and never gets to strike the piano's chords after completion. It's a misplacement of priority to invest in what you don't have the interest to explore.

I know of someone who enrolled in several certificate programs with colleges and universities in the past six years. She is yet to settle for any career. She complained of not realizing how unfit she was for most of her enrolled courses. To date, she is still searching for a career path with her continuous enrollment in new courses.

This habit has affected and restrained her from utilizing and applying most of the knowledge she has acquired over the years. Due to her constant switching from one course to another, she is yet to carve a niche for herself. Take time to look at the 4 R's you have read so far to help you remember, reflect, refill, and re-fire. The world is waiting for you.

Re-strategize

Don't back down when things go against your wish. There is no point throwing your hands in the air to declare it's all over. Certain things take time to perfect; besides, mistakes do happen. Errors are only a pointer to let us know that we can explore other options to arrive at a successful end. Always develop new strategic plans to carry on whenever you collide with challenges.

As an entrepreneur, I have had to re-strategize on countless occasions, especially in my early days in business. There were several changes I had to implement to ensure that I came out successful. Although some of the plans were not palatable to follow through; however, I had to. Some required daily, monthly, quarterly, and yearly implementation. I was able to identify and adopt the best suitable module for my business to thrive. It is not enough to develop new business strategies; we need to ensure that the approach serves its purpose. Until that is done, we may have to go back to the drawing board to re-strategize. If you carefully implement these Five R's to success, you will be amazed at the magnitude of its sustainable results.

CHAPTER 10

Tragedy of Isolation

> *There's a limit to how strong you can be. Everyone breaks when it comes to isolation because no one is stronger than loneliness; it breaks you beyond repair*
> —*Unknown*

There is no self-sufficient human. Everyone is born to support and to be supported by someone because our lives are interwoven. If you are currently reading this book, it is a proof that I had you in mind when I wrote it. The world may appear big but may not be as big as you think. Reading this book from any part of the world is a clear indication that the world is indeed small. You cannot live for yourself; neither can you be everything to yourself. We need each other to survive.

There are lots of items at your disposal when you look around your surroundings. You may or may not have a clue of when and how it was produced, yet someone chose to design it for your consumption. That designer knew how beneficial it would be to you. For instance, the manufacturers of the phones we use; had us in mind.

Without our patronage, the manufacturers would be out of business. And without the manufacturers of the phone, our communication would have been delayed. A producer without a consumer will be short-lived and will eventually go out of business. Designers and manufacturers need consumers for sustainability and continuity. The same applies to the consumers; without the manufacturers, the consumers will be without products.

The producer and consumer concept

When I started my first international business, the anxiety of not having clients show up in the first few months was unbearable. The fear of having the centre closed if no one showed up was quite scary. But thankfully, we did not get to the point of closure when clients began to come. Those clients needed our services just as much as we needed them to thrive. Without them, our presence would be meaningless. The same applies to other services; there would be no doctors without patients; likewise, no teachers without students. And, without you, this whole writing would have been a waste of my time.

Think for a while, who are your target audience when it comes to rendering services? How well do you serve them? You can only survive and thrive in what you do when people come back for more of your services and products. A one-time service plan places you in a tight corner. That is why it is critical to creating satisfaction and impression in the heart of those you serve. This concept is what makes client come back to you for more, which gives room for continuous progress. Providing service to others and being served by others makes the world go round.

In my early days in business, I remembered investing a large sum of money in starting a bead-making business. I was carried away by the beauty of the beads I handcrafted and believed that the business would boom. I did not spend time to research the demand and business module. I was utterly disappointed due to the poor patronage after I started, which led to the closure of the business. I counted my losses and moved on. To date, I still have some of those beads in my possession. That was the price I paid for neglecting the input of my intended clients. Maybe if I had taken the time to involve them in the process, their feedback would have given me a clearer picture of whether to invest in bead-making or not.

One of the reasons I failed was because I unintentionally ignored them and did not investigate the product's viability. I came up with the bead-making concept on the assumption that there would be a demand for it without considering the location and people. The idea was all about me and not about those I intended to serve, and I lost out completely. Creating services on your terms without asking for input from the end-users could lead to loss of resources and low patronage.

We stand to lose when we don't bring people on board. I remember when my spouse presented a gift of a purse to me on one of my birthdays; he was overly excited in doing so. He probed when he noticed the look on my face. I wasn't happy because I disliked many things about the purse; the shape, colour, and size. The fact is that he bought what he liked and felt I should have liked it as well. We could not exchange the purse due to the location difference, and I ended up giving it away after several months of not using it.

Sometimes, we do things hoping to be applauded, and when that doesn't happen, we become frustrated, angry, and fret. Pause and have a rethink, did you carry out a mini research to find out if your line of services and products are in demand? Carrying out research may not require much. It could be by asking questions to know how to provide services to people without guessing. This mitigates creating a self-centred product or service.

Isolation distinguished

Isolation varies; there are lots of factors that could be responsible for the different forms of isolation. Some people want to be alone in order to relax, as we saw in Chapter Eight of this book - *Just Breathe*. They want to be away from friends, colleagues, and the noise around them. To some others, isolation could emerge due to events like anger, grief, self-development, and other circumstances. Isolating yourself to rejuvenate is great. But long-term isolation, whether from yourself or others, can be harmful to your health.

There are good and bad sides to being alone, depending on the context. We may have knowingly or unknowingly experienced it at some point. Even though it has its setbacks, it can also lead to progress.

In Chapter One, I mentioned how spending time alone with yourself could lead to self-discovery. This form of isolation encourages advancement and personal development.

I deployed this form of isolation to write this book because it required me to concentrate and to be attentive. Likewise, for you to be able to read this book up to this point, you also needed this form of isolation. It is known to be a voluntary seclusion; a time set aside by you, for yourself alone and could be perceived as the feeling of loneliness and social disconnection. It is critical to use this isolation method to complete tasks. This is usually self-inflicted and does not harm. It gives us time to reflect and work towards achieving our goals.

On the other hand, seclusion, known as loneliness, can be attributed to a state of social disconnection from people. This can negatively affect you in many ways and could lead to a mental breakdown such as: sadness, depression, and anxiety. Nowadays, loneliness is more prevalent in our society than it was in the past. Daily, human interactions and connections are replaced by machines and sophisticated electronic gadgets, which makes communication more rigid.

Face-to-face communication is rapidly depreciating. It makes it harder to invest time and energy in real social relationships. When people are neglected continuously based on this, they are forced to make alternate choices. This form of isolation should be discouraged.

Socially present but absent-minded

Isolation continues to appear in different forms and intervals in our lives. Being socially present but physically disconnected happens very often. It could be caused by our environment, activities, or lack of the right companion. It is usual for one to be socially present but mentally disconnected at the same time.

The tension of life sometimes exposes us to this form of isolation. This happens to me when my emotional and physical state is affected. When we are tired, it shows up in our conversations and events; rather than engage, we yawn and nap in between. We also experience this when we are not at peace, like meeting deadlines; this often makes us spend time brainstorming on ideas rather than being fully present to socialize and engage.

Sometimes, people struggle to take their eyes off their phone to make physical connections during social gatherings like parties and conferences. These people can be physically present but absent-minded. Their actions can cost them the opportunities to connect with people. You may not know who are seated next with; it could be a potential client or business partner. Consciously make out time and effort to communicate and connect with people whenever the opportunity arises; avoid being socially blinded.

Admittedly, some of us play the victim when we are socially disengaged. We may come up with statements like "No one wants to talk to me, nobody looked in my direction when I walked into the hall, who knows, and maybe they don't like my presence." Who cares? You owe yourself the responsibility to make life worth living and to stay happy. For the most part, some people act this way to justify this form of isolation. Life can be lived with ease, and above all, try as much as possible to make it work in your favour.

The choice to make life complicated or straightforward is within our power. The way to break this social barrier is to initiate the moves and be the change. According to Mahatma Gandhi: *Be the change that you wish to see in the world.* Take the initiative to look at someone's direction if no one looked at yours. If nobody talked to you, talk to someone. If no one showed you love, then show someone some love. You can design your life the way you want it to play out. Always make a conscious effort to be fully present.

Isolations from others

There are some things you cannot control, and to such, let it be. Give your strength to the things you can control. You have minimal control over this form of isolation especially when people decide to isolate you for reasons best known to them. This isolation can happen to you anywhere: in your place of work, family, friends, and acquaintances; and can come from anyone. Some of the factors responsible for it could be race, age, gender, culture, or language barriers. Try to place a check to shake off this isolation to ward off the feeling of rejection, depression, and victimization.

Conversely, failure to nip it as soon as it appears could result in low self-esteem. When you know that you have minimal control over some circumstances, rather than go through psychological torture, it is best to create an exit point from such an environment. Furthermore, you can choose to walk away or confront the situation. Don't permit people to toy with your self-worth or bring you down. Besides, it could be particularly challenging; when there is nothing much you can do about such circumstances. However, you can strategically avoid this form of isolation by deliberately developing a unique strategy to deal with it.

The pain of isolation

Unmerited isolation is exceptionally devastating, with the potency of breaking you to your bone. More so, it causes physical, emotional, mental, and psychological trauma. This isolation leaves us with a feeling of vulnerability and insecurity, resulting in withdrawals and repulsive behaviours. Depending on the intensity of the pain, it may lead to sleeplessness, frustration, resentment, bitterness, depression, or anger. I have been inflicted time and time again by this damaging pain.

As a new immigrant, I went through some form of painful isolation, especially when I had to reject myself even before being rejected by others. I have done this on many occasions. Sometimes, before appearing for an interview, I will conclude upfront that there is no way I would qualify for the job. I did this due to lack of self-confidence. It is often expected for people to isolate us, but when we are the culprit of our own isolation, it stings so hard and hurts deeply because it provides habitation for stagnation.

I remember enrolling for a course I felt very unsuitable for, not because I was told, but it was out of my assumption. This situation inflicted so much pain on me that I spent days wishing for the course to be over because I felt out of place. As classes progressed, I became tongue-tied during discussions, even when I had valuable contributions to make. I was consumed by unnecessary fear and anxiety.

Ending the cycle of isolation

Unhealthy seclusion should be nipped urgently; the more it lingers, the more damaging it can become. What you permit, takes root, and grows; take the initiative to stop unhealthy isolation. If you are already inflicted by one, take a break to reflect and think of ways to move past it. Ask yourself these questions:

- Why am I being isolated by people?
- Why am I isolating myself?
- What can I do to stop unhealthy isolation?

Using your answers, develop a strategy to break free from it.

If you frequently feel isolated by others, look inward, and check if there is anything you can do to address it from your end. Try out new stuff to find out if you can break those barriers. Learn to strike and sustain conversations; ask questions for clarity. Boost your social skills to create opportunities for new connections. Sometimes, the problem might not be about others but with you. Try to identify and solve the problem because you need people just as much as they need you. "A tree can never make a forest," this adage was often said to me by my mother, and I find it extremely useful and rewarding when addressing unhealthy isolation.

Having people in your life is necessary and so, endeavour to maintain healthy relationships. Do everything humanly possible to avoid unhealthy isolation. Treat those who come your way with respect, regardless of their status. Abstain from taking relationships for granted. It is much harder to fix a broken relationship than it is to maintain a healthy one.

Hurts and betrayals are common factors in human relationships. Refuse to allow it to deter you from having regard for people and relationships. If you understand the law of winning and losing, you will not allow disappointments of any sort from people to take you unawares or dampen your spirit. It's not every connection that's worth strengthening or keeping; fix the ones you can and let go of the ones you cannot mend. I often hear people say: "choose your battles," not every battle is worth fighting. "You might win the battle but lose the war." Strive to be at peace with people whenever you can. Build a strong network. Remember, people matter, and you will always need them in every sphere of your life.

CHAPTER 11

Seasons

> All seasons have something to offer —Jeannette Walls

Life is short! Time flies! Seasons change! Someday, we will all run out of time. Life is a mystery. It is like a clock that ticks forward and never returns backward.

One day, every child will become a youth, every youth will become an adult, and every adult will become a senior. Eventually, every senior will pass. That is just the cycle of life.

Life is like a tree that begins as seedling, metamorphoses, and buds, and then continues into maturity with, flowers, leaves, and fruits. However, not all fruit survives to its ripened stage. Some may fall to the ground at their tender stage. So also, are the flowers, and leaves. Seasons are incredibly unpredictable. They come and go and appear only for a while. Live life to the fullest in any of the seasons you find yourself, knowing that they don't last forever. Be strategic in your plans and make informed decisions in every step of the way.

Age counts

Do you take note of some job description posts on the internet? If you do, you will find wordings like, "Applicants must be between eighteen and forty years of age." The question is, why is it important for recruiters to clearly state the age of applicants? This is often due to the nature of the job, which may require physical abilities and agility. Some recruiters even go as far as stating the reasons: the applicant must be able to do some heavy lifting and stand for an extended period. These are all pointers to the fact that age truly counts.

You can comfortably do some things at a younger age, and there are things you will struggle to do at a much older age. Swimming in an Olympic at the age of seventy or engaging in a high jump at eighty will only heap complications for your bones and general health. If you take stock of how you grew up, I am sure you would agree with me that it is normal for a child to cry in public. But if you do that without a valid reason as an adult, it will automatically raise concerns. Not only that, it will also attract attention and questions.

There are things you will never be comfortable doing again at some point in your life. Drinking from a baby's milk bottle as an adult is not what you would want to be seen doing. That phase of life is over. Getting engaged in the right things at the right time can add flavour and colour to your life. Do you want to start a business? Do you want to go back to school to further your education? Go ahead and do so. Time does not and will never wait for you. Everyone is entitled to a set amount of time, and so are you. How you choose to spend yours is up to you. Life is a choice, go out and make your time valuable.

Agony of pain

One afternoon in the summer of 2017, I returned home from work very exhausted. Despite my exhaustion, there were still pending chores that needed to be attended to before retiring to bed. My eyes were barely shut in sleep when my phone rang and would not stop. It was a call from one of my siblings in Nigeria. I reluctantly answered, only to be informed that my dad, the icon of the family, was severely injured. He slipped and broke his femur (thigh bone). I requested to speak with him, and from his voice, it was evident that he was in severe pain.

He tried so hard to hide the severity of his pains from me but could not do so for long. Amid our conversation, he broke down in tears but quickly apologized for invading my world with his predicament. This made me wonder, did dad have to apologize? I could sense the magnitude of the pain in his voice. His constant groaning all through our conversation tore me apart. I could no longer hold back my emotions and broke down in tears at my end. For the first time, dad sounded weak and helpless; that stung me beyond description. I wept for him; the pillar of the family was now dependent. How ironic! How the one time very strong man has suddenly become weak. Tables do turn. He ended the call with a huge sigh.

Dad was always there for me as a child, and I believe it was my turn to be there for him in his old age, especially now that he needed me the most. Besides, his predicament demanded my availability irrespective of the distance that separated us. His current state of health was no fault of his and was beyond his control. Dad and Mom have been there for my siblings and me, through thick and thin. It was time for us to show them love in this critical season of their lives.

He is eighty years old, and there is not so much he can do about his health. The pain of a broken femur at his age has been quite challenging, which resulted in a major surgery. Although the operation was successful, however, it left him in severe pain and stress. He is no longer his bubbly self. Pain has a way of holding someone down behind bars. After the surgery, his health deteriorated, and he has not been the same since then.

On several occasions, he has made numerous attempts to walk a few times and fell. These days, he hardly takes step without pain and tears. His bones have suddenly grown weak by the day, and his strength can no longer carry him as it did in the past. Moreover, considering his age, the healing process has been awfully slow. A few days ago, I was informed that he was confined to a wheelchair. Hearing this broke my heart to bits and made me wonder if dad will ever progress past this phase. When I think of his former agility and confinement to a wheelchair, I cannot imagine what the future holds for him.

My father, my faith legend, my pathfinder, my pastor, my coach, a God sent, and the world's best mentor; I can only hope and pray for his recovery to happen soon.

My icon of faith

Despite all of these, he has refused to give up. He still pushes himself to walk unaided and has fallen many times, leaving him with more scars and pains. I believe he has given his best and has done everything within his power to walk again, but to no avail. I know age is no longer on his side, and I am proud of his numerous efforts to help himself stand on his feet again. Sadly, some seasons come with untold hardships. With his failing health, I am forced to look back at how great a father he has been and still is. It was dad who taught me self-value and self-contentment. My father may not have given me the world, but he gave me wings to explore the world and to know that it could be mine for the taking. Today, I have soared above several storms and attained higher heights with those wings.

To my father: I remember as a child when we (my siblings and I) would come to you crying for Christmas clothes and shoes because of what our friends wore. It was you, dad, who always reminded us that "The best gift a father could give his children was his presence and not presents (physical gifts, which is only for a moment)." As I consider how great of a father you are, I am optimistic that this pain will soon fade away. I choose to look at the bright side of life with the hope that you will recover soon, and not long from now.

Mom, on the other hand, has also had her fair share of health struggles, which also comes with ageing. Seeing these two great icons go through this much pain gives me goosebumps and concerns. As a child, dad and mom were my superheroes. They were very energetic, outgoing, fun-loving, and full of life, but age has held them hostage. They have gradually taken a bow from active lifestyles. Their present health is a constant reminder that nothing in life is permanent. The cars we drive today will be old someday; the houses we live in will be outdated; our clothes and possessions will become out of fashion. Eventually, everything will fade away with time.

As it stands, I dearly hold to heart this famous saying by Joseph Smith Jr: "That which has a beginning will surely have an end." People try so hard to run away from ageing. They indulge in different things to stay forever young; they do facelifts, surgeries, enhancements, and more. These will only last for a while. Age cannot be subdued; neither can it be suppressed. When it comes to ageing, there is only a little or nothing you can do about it. You can't hide the signs; it is a matter of time before it will show up. Do make up your mind to embrace it as it comes. Age gracefully and be happy each step of the way.

Every season comes with its uniqueness, peaks, and valleys. Some seasons make you feel like a winner, while some make you feel like a loser. Tough times may appear insurmountable, but they are. As people advance in age, some may look back at how they have lived their lives and take stock of their achievements and failures. The impact they created and failed to create while they were young. This stock-taking can sometimes end in disappointment or victories.

It is difficult for some people to handle each season of their lives effectively and efficiently, while others may find it easy, and are able to transition the various decades of their sojourn here on earth. Those who have lived more than half of their lives cannot afford to waste any more time on frivolities. Use your time wisely by living a purpose-driven life. Some treat major milestones with utmost pride and respect, such as birthdays, achievements, anniversaries, wedding days, and so on. They do this to show how important these days are and spend a fortune to celebrate them. This celebration is a great concept, but also, it is important to spend a fortune to make your life count. Plan your life, having in mind that you don't have all the time in your hands.

When I first left the shores of my home country, I lived my life not knowing the essence of time. After few years, I reminisced in disappointment on how much time I expended. Those disappointments handed me a lesson on the value of time. My desire is to salvage those wasted times and to make the absolute best out of my remaining seasons.

Seasons don't last forever

Everything is anchored on seasons, and nothing exists without it. There is nothing you do that someone else has not done or attempted to do. It is common for people to aim for the skies and desire to outshine everyone else. Understand that people have gone ahead of you, and some have already achieved most of your aspirations.

The fight to surpass everyone is a constant battle that will continually rage in our minds. It could be craving to be the best in your area of expertise, maybe singing or dancing. While doing all of these, keep in mind that your attainments could be outperformed, and others will continually outshine your records.

Your much-celebrated success today could be someone else's starting point tomorrow. Most of our best clothing of yesterday no longer have space in our closet today, while some have been trashed. Our achievements will depreciate with the progress of time. Seasons don't last forever, just like anything in this world will not last forever. James

Dobson once said, "If you live long enough, life will trash your trophies."

As a teenager, I used to think that being an adult meant total freedom. I earnestly looked forward to it. Now, as an adult, I sincerely wish I could rewind the hands of time. I did not understand the responsibility that came with adulthood until I became one. It is interesting to see how the very things I took for granted, which made no sense to me as a teenager, suddenly made so much sense as an adult.

I am constantly driven to live a life of impact and exemplary life for my children. While you still have the time, make your passion a reality, write that book, get that job, build that orphanage centre, and inspire that girl, boy, woman and man. Sponsor that child through school if that is what you are compelled to do. What do you want to be said about your life at the end of your sojourn? Time is running out.

Your seasons matter

Your shining is dependent on you. You can shine at every phase of your seasons if you embrace the following principles:

- **You are all that matters**: Knowing that you are all that matters play a vital role in your journey to greatness. Nobody will ever eat or sleep for you. Knowing yourself is personal. One of the greatest gifts of a lifetime is to discover who you are. Until you have the full knowledge and understanding of yourself, you will continue to struggle. Knowing yourself begins and ends with you. Take charge of your life in order to remain relevant.

- **Embrace change**: Often, it is said that true change begins with you. There is no point in changing your associates, jobs, colleagues, and everything except yourself. True change begins with your acceptance to change. You cannot change what you don't accept. Acceptance makes change accessible and possible. Rigidity to change delays growth. Be open to new ideas and embrace new concepts.

- **Seek help**: If getting a mentor or a coach will ease your struggle to success, then, by all means, get one. Do not be afraid of asking for help. After all, everybody needs somebody. According to John Donne – "No man is an island entire of itself." We are connected to one another; a "Yes" or "No" does no harm for an answer. Those are the two responses you will always receive when you ask for help. People are either willing to help you or not. Hearing "No" should not put your life on hold. Keep moving and searching until you find or hear a "Yes." Develop the confidence and courage to seek help.

- **Gather information**: Search out information that are relevant to your progress and expose yourself to it. Knowledge is your life wire to advancement. However, not all information is meant for your consumption. Learn the act of validating the sources as it comes your way before utilizing it. Refuse to be driven around by every information. You are not a dumping ground. Pick, choose, discard, and apply correctly. Information can make you grow or bring you down.

Understanding your seasons is a vital key that can help you live a meaningful life. When you are aware of the importance of each season, you will give everything within your reach to make all your seasons meaningful.

CHAPTER 12

Cycle of Life

Life is a cycle and will remain that way; it occurs at different ages and stages over our lifespan. This cycle symbolizes the beginning and end of our journey. Everybody is bound to go through different phases in the cycle of life. Each second, minute, and hour we live is critical; it draws us closer to the end.

I still have good memories of my elementary, high school, college, and university days. They frame an integral part of my world. The day I took my marital vows and carried my children are evergreen in my memory. My last child is seven years old, and it baffles me to see how time goes by so fast. Sometimes, I ponder and ask myself, where did time go? Time surely does fly!

Any missed time in these cycles is lost because they are unique and distinct. The cycle of life is like a progressive storybook with a beginning and an end. It translates into four categories and embedded in each category is the representation of the four seasons of our lives.

- **Human:** child, youth, adult, and senior
- **Weather:** spring, summer, fall, and winter
- **Day:** morning, afternoon, evening, and night
- **Plant:** seedling, young plant, flower, and fruit

As you already saw in Chapter Eleven - Seasons, everything progresses with time. Life is like a building with an entrance and exit. Nothing in life lasts forever; a time comes when the old must give way for the new. The first season with humans begins as a child, it evolves into a youth, matures into an adult, then into a senior, and eventually fades away. We will all come face-to-face with each of this cycle. However, some may not make it round the various seasons. They may exit early, in their childhood, others in their youth, some in their adult years, while some will experience their full cycle of life. Life is short! If you live with this insight, you will fight to make every aspect relevant.

Let's carry out this exercise; shut your eyes for a minute and imagine yourself on a stage with a mandate to give your best speech in two minutes:

- What will you say?
- Do you think your message will be powerful enough to penetrate the hearts of people?
- Will it leave a lasting impression?
- Will you struggle to craft one?
- Do you think that you will find fulfilment after your speech?

As you go through life, always ensure to give your best performance irrespective of the time constraint. Often, it is not how long but how well that truly matters. Some opportunities will only come once in your lifetime. According to Chaucer, "Time and tide wait for no man." Each tick of the clock is a sign that the end is drawing nearer, and the ability to understand your cycle will give you the boost required to achieve your goals early in life.

Understanding seasons

Seasons are likened to the cycle of life; they are our lifetime companions and will always be present. They are synonymous to sunrise and sunset. The time between these two reflects the value of our time and how we lived our lives. Sunrise is a representation of our birth, which connotes our entrance into the world, while sunset mirrors our exit from this world. Strive to engrave a legacy to make a difference during these periods. Avoid time-wasting, and procrastination; be consistent in all your ways.

Never leave what you can do today for tomorrow; make the best use of your today because tomorrow may never come. Get down to business; do what you have to do now. It is time to unveil those hidden talents engraved in you. Do everything within your power to live a life of impact. As you advance in age, your bones become feeble, and you may lose the drive and stamina to carry out what you should have accomplished early in life. Now is the time to actualize your dreams. I am not sure where you belong in the four seasons of life, but the explanation below will give you an insight into each season as humans and where you perfectly fit in.

Child: morning and spring season

This is the beginning of the cycle of life. Think about your childhood and how dependent you were. You had little or no control over the things that affected your life, like the house you lived in, the vehicle you drove in, and the school you attended. The clothes and shoes you wore were all handed to you without a choice. Your parents or guardians planned everything for you at that age. The decision of when to sleep, what to eat, and when to bathe, were beyond your abilities and control.

This phase represents the morning and spring. The morning is when the child is innocent. It is the early stage of a child's life, with no scar. The springtime is a representation of the blooming phase of a child when he or she begins to bud. In this season, mistakes are bound to happen, and those mistakes are corrected with minimal or no consequences. They get all the support and attention needed to excel, even without requesting for it. This season only lasts for a while.

Youth: afternoon and summer season

Your strength is at its peak when you are a youth. This is when you begin to take responsibility and become accountable for your actions. Freedom gradually kicks in at this stage. You are slammed with consequences based on your choices. The choices you make, whether good or bad will show up at the latter part of your life. Poor choices can mar you for the rest of your life.

On the other hand, great choices can set you up for success. It is a sensitive season and is often assumed to be the most vibrant of all the four seasons. If you belong to this season, you have age and strength on your side. You have enough time to explore, make mistakes, correct, and adjust where necessary.

In this cycle of life, youth is like the afternoon and summer season. The afternoon is usually very bright; it is not too early and not too late, but simply perfect. You can achieve a lot as well as encounter numerous opportunities from all directions. Visibility is clearer; your bones are stronger, and you are filled with high level of energy.

The youth season in this context could be related to summer when outdoor activity is usually on the rise, and movement is at its peak. All these are characteristics of the life of a youth, a life filled with fun and endless opportunities. Unfortunately, some people fail to utilize the benefit that comes with this season due to distraction, peer pressure, lack of time management and lost identity. This may hinder them from making the best out of this season.

Adult: evening and fall season

This season represents adulthood. The decisions and choices one made as a youth will begin to manifest at this stage. Consequences become evident; some will either struggle or soar because of their choices. Full accountability sets in; you take actions for yourself. The decision is all yours: whether to marry or not, the kind of work you do, your choice of house and car. This responsibility does not just end with you. You no longer live for yourself alone. You are considerate and committed to your immediate and extended family, as well as your community. In this season, destinies maybe directly or indirectly connected to you; your children, siblings, aged parents, and maybe some less privileged in the society might be dependent on you.

Most people in this season unknowingly run round in circles serving others and unintentionally forget to take care of themselves. They get busy at the expense of planning for their future and retirement. Some of them may find out later in life that engaging in many activities is not equivalent to productivity and accomplishments.

The pressures and distractions associated with this phase of life could lead to a lifetime of emptiness. It is crucial to be attentive to how you spend your time; if not, you may realize later that you expended it disproportionately. The evening is when the day gradually starts to get dark, and vision is not as clear as during the time of youth and afternoon stage—these transitions into the nighttime season — senior.

Senior: night and winter season

This is an indication of the night season. Arriving at this season is a journey; one must have had the opportunity and privilege of experiencing the other three seasons. For some, the night or winter season creeps in unannounced. Notwithstanding, it comes with some signals: The body gives signs of fragility; vision grows dim. The struggle with actively engaging in the things that one could do with ease begins to set in, like running, heavy lifting, and climbing. It ushers in the retirement phase and marks the beginning of the end of the cycle of life. This is the last and final of all the seasons; it is very crucial and should be given maximum attention. Although your agility is gradually slowing down, you can still add colour to your life and flavour to those around you. You may be at the nighttime of your life as a senior but not knocked out; you are still capable of touching lives.

Carry out a soul search. What do you have inside of you that can potentially be a blessing to others? Rather than box-in all your expertise, you can choose to off-load them. You have significant experiences to hand down. The choice is all yours; decide to share your experiences and lessons from each season with the younger generation to guide them through life. Be deliberate in engaging in activities that will rejuvenate your mind to keep you fit.

Take care of your health. Exercise to stay active and read books to keep your mind refreshed. If possible, volunteer to build connections with people and your community. Acting as a coach or mentor to someone younger can help exercise your brain. Belonging to social groups could also help keep loneliness and isolation at bay.

If you are unable to find any activity or volunteering groups that suit your style, then create one. Even though this season can sometimes be tough, refuse to render yourself redundant. Do the things that stimulate you, maintain a positive outlook, and try as much as possible to be happy with yourself. Take out time to relax.

It is the night season of life. In this phase, everything slows down; drivers drive with caution. This season can lead to depression if not carefully managed. It symbolizes the winter season when roads are usually slippery, and vehicles go slow due to impending hazards. People are careful of every step they take to avoid falling. It reflects the life of a senior and marks the end of the final stage in the cycle of life.

Leave historical record

Each cycle occurs once in our lifetime. Our experience with these cycles: child, youth, adult, and senior are only a one-time affair. The greatest lesson to take home is; a meaningful life is not in the number of your days here on earth, but in the legacy you imprinted, the lives you touched and above all, how well you lived.

It is beyond our capability to rewind the hands of the clock. No one lives forever. Improve upon your yesterday; make today your best day and your future filled with hope. Strive to create historical records early because time will continue to tick and kick forward.

Do not spend all your time counting your years, seasons, and assets, but rather, make every season of your life worth living. Inspire people to take the right action to fulfill their purpose. All my life, I did not imagine that one day, I would become a public speaker or an author; neither did I intend to own a childcare centre, but my experiences in life inspired me to do the things I do. Those actions I took have led me to where I am today and will continue to lead me to where I will be tomorrow. My goal is to ensure that my cycle of life is purposeful. You can make your life meaningful.

CHAPTER 13

Carve the Path

> *Life is either a daring adventure or nothing at all —*
> *Helen Keller*

Initially, when I set out to write this book, I was afraid that no one would read it. The thought of writing it gave way to anxiety. I was not sure if anyone would be willing to flip through the pages, neither was I sure if I would have the right words to complete it. These thoughts and questions raced through my mind for a long time. But look! You are not only flipping through the pages; you have been patient enough to read up to this point. Writing this book was one of my biggest tests of leaving a legacy and footprints to inspire people to create a successful path in their lives, business, and career.

In this chapter - Carve your Path, represents your products and services. I will start by asking a few questions. What can you do to serve humanity? How can you be a change agent in the world? Keep in mind that when you rise, those around you are lifted as well. You can choose to carve a path in any area of your life no matter how small, whether in dancing, as an artist, or going back to school. Your future lies within your grasps. Carving your path can be contagious enough to inspire others to also carve a path for themselves.

My achievements once inspired someone to say, "Vicky, if you can accomplish all these: being a founder of a childcare learning centre, writing books, a public speaker, coaching and mentoring thousands of people across the globe, then you have challenged me to chase after my dreams." Today, she is the founder of a learning institute for training teachers in Africa. She drew inspiration from my attainments and got motivated, and currently, she is living her dreams. I am sure her success will also inspire someone else to take action in bringing their dreams to fruition.

I remember attending a conference where a friend of mine was the keynote speaker. She was very phenomenal on stage, and her speech was top-notch. Her actions inspired me to offload what I had bottled up for years. I was motivated by her achievements to start my public speaking career. Doing big stuff is great, but when carving a path, little things also matter.

The things you consider little could be someone else's big stuff, and what you believe to be big could be someone else's little stuff. Singing might seem so little to you but could be a big deal to someone else. Acquiring a parachute might mean the world to someone but might not intrigue you. As you set out to manoeuvre your path to success, bear in mind that making impact comes in different shades. Whether big or small, the bottom line is for you to inspire people to excel at any level.

Make an entrance

Just like any path would need an entrance, every business also needs an entrance. Be accessible; make it easy for people to benefit from what you have to offer. People are resentful when they have to go through a series of barricades to gain access to your product and services. What skills do you possess? What are your products and services? How easy is it for people to lay hold of it? You cannot have an in-demand service, and then, make people wait for a long time before they can access your services.

No one would want to go through the hassle of driving around before being able to gain entry to any business premises. It will spur them to look for an alternative if they find it difficult to get in. Set up viable systems and structures to facilitate efficiency and effectiveness in any services rendered. This is what attracts and retains people. It is great to have products and services, but don't make people detest what you do because of poor service quality.

My son's barber is an expert at what he does but struggles to keep up with the demand. Irrespective of how early I set up an appointment to meet with him, it never works. He strolls in late, between eleven in the morning and noon each time I visit. I have had to give up my spots on several occasions or wait for more than one to two hours to be able to have access to his services. I got fed up and resented by his business module. I have since moved on, and I am sure; others with similar experiences must have moved on too. Although he is great at what he does, however, I see a business that is short-lived, except there is a drastic change in his systems and structural setup.

The entrance to a path is an open invitation for anyone to tread or drive through it. A business without a strategic approach would not last. In life, your expertise, who you are, what you do, and how you do the things you do, are all the entrances that lead to your products and services. They are your gateway to greatness. Your entrance is linked to your brand. Seek to create a remarkable impression on those who access your services and products.

The concepts

A few years ago, I received a letter in my mailbox about an upcoming development project in the community I lived in. Attached was a map with a detailed description and an image of what the upcoming development would look like. I could see shopping malls, houses, offices, schools, recreational centres, and other complexes in the picture. If there were no roads on the diagram, I would have been disturbed by a potential defect in the plan. The integrity of the project would have been questioned, and the possibility of completing and gaining entry to those buildings would have been flawed.

Thankfully, the drawings on the map were more detailed. It included entrances, both major and minor roads, as well as designs for pathways and footpaths. This clearly showed the importance of entrances, roads, pathways, and signs. When construction began, I took a keen interest in the different phases of the projects. All through the process, I was attentive to the progress of the building each time I drove past. I did this to gain a clear insight into how the project was being executed.

From mapping to edifice

When construction began, the entrances and roads were the very first thing I saw the workers map out before commencing work on the structures. It was through the mapped-out routes that all the construction work gained traction for the successful completion of the development. Workers and building equipment were able to gain access to their various sites through the entrances and roads. Currently, that project is completed, and it's a masterpiece. It has added beauty to the community. A vast number of people go in and out of the area daily. Those beautiful structures have automatically added value as well as opened the area to many activities. This has led to the establishment of many new businesses and career opportunities.

The description on the diagram gave the community a mental picture of how the project would look like upon completion. Sometimes, we have a mental picture of who we want to become, where we want to be and how we want to get there; but somehow, we get lost by the complexities in the process. When this happens, reminisce on Chapter Ten - Tragedy of Isolation. No one is a master of all, reach out to someone who has a blueprint, and who is more knowledgeable to help you move past that phase.

Helping someone carve a successful path is everybody's call. Yes, that is true; you just read it. Did I hear you say you have nothing to offer? Or you don't know how to help? That is not true! You just did! By reading this book, you have helped me to fulfill one of my numerous purposes in life. You just carved a path of impact for me. First, you must believe that you have something to offer, and the rest will follow. And then, dig deep to discover what you have to serve humanity. Whether it is giving someone a smile or a pat on the back, just go ahead and do it.

Don't look down on yourself; reject the feeling of emptiness. Unveil those suppressed potentials and allow it to flow freely. Walk with your head held high because you can be a change-agent in the world. We cannot continue to ignore and watch our gifting go to waste; we have allowed many to rot away already. It is time to salvage what we have left within us.

The process of carving a path

I have experienced different shifts in an attempt to serve humanity, part of which has led me to burn the midnight candle. On several occasions, I was stricken with hunger, not because I had no food, but because I was consumed with a passion for helping others carve their path to success. There were also times I deprived myself of some social gatherings due to time constraints with the busy tasks at hand. During this time, I lost some close allies because I was unable to keep up with their constant demand for my presence. And they on the other hand, could not relate to the fact that I was called to serve at a higher level and needed to be of service.

Serving people can be exceptionally challenging. Sometimes, I experience heartbreaks when the result doesn't seem to add up. At such moments, it makes me doubt and question the integrity of my capabilities. Carving a path might not always go in line with your desired outcome. A few issues here and there could question the integrity of your knowledge. Amid all these, stand firm and let determination be your watchword.

Leave footprints

> *The sky is not the limit...there are footprints on the moon. No dream is too high* — Buzz Aldrin

You can leave a footprint in the sands of time. There are still many paths to be carved, people to be served, and more bridges to be built. Most roads have landmarks and signs to make the journey worthwhile and memorable. You too can make somebody's life worthwhile.

Life will be blissful if we are instrumental in carving a path of service for ourselves and others. Take and own the responsibility of being your brother's keeper, if you must serve, do it wholeheartedly. Endeavour to make the world a better place than you met it. Aspire to leave an unforgettable experience in someone's life. Always give your best; you never know whose life it will impact and where they will end up.

Be a bridge

As a bridge, you connect others to opportunities. We often fail to look at the big picture when we render services to people. The reality is that, at first, it may appear as if you are serving others, but in the end, you will realize that in serving others, you were directly or indirectly serving yourself. Continue to be of service to people; it could be of immense benefit to you one day. Search and identify ways to bridge gaps.

I wrote this book with the hope of inspiring someone, but I ended up inspiring myself. By reading this book, you have inspired me to write more books. Besides, it has added value to who I am today. You don't lose what you give; it will surely find a way of returning to you. It may be in a different way, but it will surely come back to you. Good deeds never go unrewarded. Always give your best. My desire was to be a source of blessing to others, but in return, I was exposed to a new world of leadership and opportunities.

This experience has taught me that; the more I am of service to others, the more my knowledge broadens. Serving has helped me empty myself for others to be full, and somehow, I have found a way of constantly refilling myself. When you become a bridge to connect others to their blessings, in like manner, blessings will also find a way of reaching you.

From trials to pathfinder

I have seen and read a lot about people who rose from nothing to something, failure to fame, and from rags to riches. They did not just stumble on success; they worked extremely hard to turn their struggles into breakthroughs. Their trials, rejections, sleepless nights, and tears have a way of inspiring me. I get inspired by another peculiar set of people, those who were born into fame and riches, and are still able to uphold the blueprint of success.

Maintaining and not letting go of successful track records is one of the most challenging things to do. People who are on the verge of rising to their limelight; fight extremely hard to keep their hopes and dreams alive. These people challenge me too. I believe everyone has what it takes to contribute to the growth of humanity.

Today, I do the things I do because of those who are successful and those who are currently on their journey to success. I am where I am because of both the weak and strong and those who have failed and risen. I have soared on different wings to get to this height of attainment. Although I may not have many achievements under my wings; however, I am willing to serve humanity with what I have. Success and greatness are all entwined in service. They usually come to us as blessings in disguise when we make ourselves available to be of service to others.

I met a lady whose job was to ensure that the washrooms were cleaned and maintained daily. The way and manner she carried out her tasks with smiles gave me a different perception to life. She would stop in her tracks with a huge smile to say hello to anyone who came in to use the washroom. Those smiles meant so much to me; I learned from her disposition to be cheerful when rendering services of any kind. It is commonly said, "There is dignity in labour." This lady is also a part of my success story.

In life, I draw knowledge from different people. Some say, "Variety is the spice of life." Nobody should be relegated to the background, despite their status or level of attainment. Treat everyone that crosses your way with utmost respect; you may be in an obscured angle to be able to predict what tomorrow would unfold. Time and events may change the trajectory of life.

I learn from people who have risen above their failure; they taught me that no condition is permanent. Those who are weak made me understand that being weak; is not equivalent to failure. I have learned to see the good and beauty in people in whatever phase of life they are in, whether rich or poor. They motivate and inspire me in their own unique ways. I live my life being inspired by ordinary people in peculiar circumstances. Refuse to allow your gifting die in your hands. Giving a piece of yourself for others to excel does not make you small; it will only elevate you.

CHAPTER 14

Perform to Rule

> All the world's a stage, And all the men and women merely players; They have their exits and entrances, And one man in his time plays many parts —William Shakespeare

The words perform, and to rule requires action to make it a complete process. Everyone is born and wired to perform knowingly or unknowingly. It is beyond our power to decide whether to act or not. Someone reading this might choose to say, "No," I'm not a performer. Do you know that by saying "No" is an act on its own, and that makes you a performer?

Whether you choose to remain silent, passive, actively engaged, or just watch, it does not alter the fact that you are a performer. Each of these acts could be intentional or unintentional. From the time we wake up to the time we retire to our beds, we are frequently involved in one activity or the other. Even while sleeping, we are still acting, we roll from one side of our beds to the other, move our legs, hands, and sleeping position unconsciously. Even though some of our acts are unintentional, however, we can intentionally control the outcome of our performances. Newborn babies begin to perform and rule from the day they are born. They cry, suck, gently move their hands, and kick their legs to seek attention. These acts enable them to express themselves in a manner that results in feeding, diapering, or a cuddle depending on their needs. Their performance attracts attention and gives them the power to rule their world. For instance, when a baby cries, it commands attention and moves those around the baby into action. Most parents, guardians, loved ones would do everything within their power to soothe their baby. Newborns perform effortlessly and naturally without minding the outcome. Both babies and adults perform without a physical stage with a limited audience, unlike professional performers who are intentional with a physical stage and sometimes large audience.

Babies usually begin with unintentional acts, but as they grow older, they evolve and become aware of the powers of their performance and use it to their advantage. As time progresses, some of their performances become targeted. They can decide to stage a superb act by throwing tantrums just to have their way. It may be through intensified cry to get the desired attention to meet their needs.

My son at fifteen-months of age was an expert in pulling a superlative performance that would make us run helter-skelter in different directions. He was the best at what he does, crying. He could go on for as long as he deemed it fit without taking a break. On one occasion, I remember when we; my husband, his siblings and I, had to race into a shop in search of a mouth pacifier.

He woke up from sleep while we were driving home to discover that he did not have a pacifier in his mouth to suck upon, and this got him upset, and he began to cry. After pacifying him for nearly thirty minutes to calm him, he bluntly refused to budge. The only option left was to get him one in order to have our sanity back. Now, as I look back in humour, I cannot help but reel out with laughter at such a powerful and magnificent performance just to get his pacifier back. I am sure that some of you with babies might relate to this.

As adults, we perform without limits every second, minute, hour, day, week, month, and year. We act for different audiences, both known and unknown, without restriction. You are in charge of what you do and, how you want your performance to begin and end is dependent on you. It's either you are ruling your world with an unparallel performance, or the world will rule you. You can choose to leave a remarkable impression or a sour trail whenever you perform.

We hop on many stages in a day to carry out distinctive acts, and we are constantly switching from one role to another. If you are a mother, a wife, or a teacher, your act varies from time to time and from place to place. You will wear different hats and function in different capacities: mom to your children, wife to your husband, a colleague or boss at your place of work.

Your stages of performance

Your stage is everywhere, your kitchen, living room, office, social media, church, school, business arena, restaurant, the list goes on. These are all places to showcase your conducts, skills and how you perform. It houses your acts. Right where you are, with this book, is your stage, and you are carrying out an act by reading. Let us quickly go through the question route to enable us gain clarity of this chapter. Pause for a moment and try to answer these questions:

- Do you have a job? If your answer is yes, your place of work is your stage. That is where you need to give your best performance to your assigned task
- Are you a business owner? If your answer is also yes; you have a stage right there in your business premises which includes how you serve your clients
- Are you a homemaker, a wife, or a mother? Ensure that everything about your home is splendid because that is your stage

Any time you have the privilege of working anywhere, understand that you are putting up a show or selling your value for people to see. People usually describe us by the things they see us do.

I remember someone referring to me as the lady who teaches children how to read some time ago. That was a description of me by virtue of what I did. Have you not heard people say things like, "The man who sings or the woman who dances?" Some people go as far as qualifying the performance. For instance, you hear them say stuff like

"The man who sings very well or the lady who is extremely good at dancing." People gain or lose out of great opportunities when the description of what they do is flawed. Those who leave a review or refer clients to you do so base on your performance. Reviews are either good or bad. Try as much as you can to perform at your peak level whenever you show up. Someone somewhere might be watching you and will remember you by your peak or low conduct. Give a "Wow" performance at all times.

Being recommended for an admission or a job does not imply an automatic acceptance. And even if you are accepted, the real you will manifest after a while. What this means is that your conduct, values, and ethics will come to light sooner or later. Sadly, a lot of people abuse or blow off their privileges of being recommended. As a result, they shut the door of opportunities, not only to themselves but to others as well.

My second book, "Lessons From Trailblazers," is an anthology, a collection of stories from twenty-three different everyday people who turned their trials to triumph. Some of those who were recommended to take part in the writing did not gain a spot in the book irrespective of the recommendation from respected individuals. What they represented did not rest well with the project based on what I gathered from the online background check I conducted.

Your space and your brand

We live in an era where people watch, observe, and draw conclusions about who you are from a distance and from different mediums. The majority of what you post, like, share, re-share, and tweet about on social media, reveals and tells a story about you. I have friends who sell fabric, cosmetics, foodstuffs, coaching packages, and supplements on social media platforms. None of them called or sent a message to inform me of what they do; it is all out there on their social media pages. By looking at their posts and messages, I can confidently conclude on who they are and their values. I knew who and what my coach represented on social media before I connected with her.

We have in-depth knowledge of people by what they portray in their social space. I have had to send congratulatory messages to people due to their posts and got to discover that they were not the original owner. But they failed to acknowledge that the posts were not theirs. It is critical to note that whatever you post is traceable to you. Some get tagged on nearly everything by strangers, without consent, and yet they have no clue about it.

When people go to your social media platform to view your profile, what do you think will pop up when your name is typed in the search engine? What comes up says a lot about you. You might not have the chance to explain how those posts showed up on your page. Even when you are not active on social media, for the fact that you created an account under your name is enough reason for you to take charge of your page.

There is nothing much you can do to control some of these excesses; however, do the little you can. Be very vigilant; look out for yourself. Some people may stop at your social space only once, and the impression they receive can either attract or repel them from visiting again.

I was very negligent of mine in the past. Strangers and the people I knew took over my page with their tags and posts. Have you ever opened your page only to be bombarded by different posts that made you feel like a stranger in your own space? Posts that are not in line with who you are, and your belief can contradict what you represent. When you allow your social media platforms to be used as a dumping ground for all sorts of posts in the name of tagging, it will swallow up your brand, identity, and values. It creates confusion and reduces your visibility and spheres of influence.

With time, I have gotten better with the functionalities on social media. These days, I try as much as possible to show up on my platforms with excellent performance because that is one of the ways I can rule my world. I see people ruling theirs through a superlative performance on social media without a physical stage. Those who provide services like selling of products, speaking engagements, or coaching earn a living and create impacts via this avenue. Currently, I take a daily tour around all my platforms to ensure that there is no inappropriate post on my page from strangers or friends.

Sometimes, I have had to send private messages to some of my allies who are in the habit of dumping stuff on my wall as precautionary measures. And outrightly**,** I have also had to block some strangers who are a nuisance; I pull down and block posts that are not aligned with my principles.

As an educational consultant, a lot of people have reached out to me for mentoring and coaching as a result of my educational posts. These are people I have never met, but social space brought us together. My brand and what I represent was the key attraction.

Here are some critical questions to ponder about; these questions will expose you to areas in your life that can be improved upon to help you render a powerful performance.

- Why are you on social media?
- Why do you follow people on social platform?
- What gets you easily put off?
- Why are you attracted to some people?
- Do you pay attention to every post on social media?
- What makes you comment, tweet, share, or re-share posts?
- Can you confidently say that you are creating impact?
- What are your posts targeted at?
- Who are your posts meant for?
- Have you ever searched for your name on Google search engine?
- If yes, what does the search on Google says about you?

The world has transformed significantly; people see and observe what you do before they are attracted to you for a physical or social connection. Whether you like it or not, you are frequently judged by what you display; and you may most likely judge others by what they do and display as well. Gone are the days when one could boldly say: "I can act, say, and post whatever I want, it doesn't matter." No! Anything you do, say, or post these days truly matters; they count. The world has gone past that level. Your actions will either stand against you or for you. A lot of people and big organizations have gone extinct because of poor conduct and performances in public.

Do you know right now, there are lots of business transactions taking place on social media among strangers? They have never met before but are connected based on their interest and values. Are you aware that people gain employment online? People also get rejected due to their negative conduct online. Be prepared because most people will check you out online before committing their time and resources to engage in anything serious with you. Great performers are those who have mastered their acts and can retain and bring in audiences to watch them shine in their acts.

Don't live a life of "whatever will be, will be." Strategically position yourself for opportunities. Success does not thrive in a casual environment; you must prepare to meet with it. There is no coincidence when it comes to achieving greatness; you work for it. There are names you can count on in some sports: in soccer, you hear of names like Lionel Messi and Neymar Jr. In basketball, you will hear of Michael Jordan, Stephen Curry, and in lawn tennis, names like Serena Williams, Novak Djokovic, and many other great names. How did they arrive at where they are? Their performance paved the way for them to be a reference and household names.

A one-time performance is not enough to carry you through. If you must continually be a sought-after, then you must consistently stand out in whatever you do. Strive to leave people with a memorable impression. People, who usually showcase top-notch acts, often play their hearts out to remain relevant and to continually retain their spots. Nobody loves to be replaced by someone else in their field of expertise. Great acts can catapult you to the right place at the right time.

Behind-the-scenes

In the words of the wise, "There is time for everything under the sun." A child does not progress from crawling to jumping without going through the full cycle of movement. If he does, he will crash. It is not every act that is meant for public eyes at the first instant. Some would need to be nurtured and mastered before being exposed.

Before introducing this book to the public, I went through different processes: drafting, editing, proofreading, typesetting, cover design, and marketing. Imagine if I published the manuscript without going through those processes. It would have been a total disaster with lots of unclear messages filled with errors, typos, and misunderstanding. This book and my authority would have been questionable.

Be diligent enough to know when to groom yourself behind-the-scenes to avoid struggles. In order to perfect an act, people need a behind-the-scene experience. The athlete, singer, drummer, and student will have to go through this experience to pull off a phenomenal performance. Behind-the-scenes is where skills are perfected; errors are corrected, and champions are born. It is a costly and sacrificial place.

A student whose desire is to become a doctor does not just boldly declare, "I am a doctor." A lot would have been addressed behind-the-scenes before the open declaration. That student must have been involved with several years of studies, sleepless nights, exams, internships, and more before he can publicly and confidently confess to being a doctor.

A friend of mine went through a series of layoffs in her place of work because she voluntarily assumed roles that exposed her deficiencies and inexperience. To be daring is an excellent attribute to have but being daring without being aware of one's boundaries and limitations will only end in frustration. Staying behind-the-scenes does not make you less important or weak. Rather, it empowers and gives you time to grasp and master your acts before making any public appearance. Behind-the-scenes is the powerhouse of every outstanding performer.

Understanding when to operate from the background is very crucial. Don't be in a hurry to launch that business, vision, or services; be patient enough to work from the background to perfect your acts.

Audience

Your audience is everywhere, just like your stage is everywhere; in malls, gyms, schools, offices, home, and anywhere you find yourself. Their role is to watch you perform. It is beyond your control to pick and choose your audience or those you want to watch you. However, the ability to control your performance is yours. Whether you like it or not, you will always be watched. Those who watch you are there to give you feedback, recommend, and refer people to you. See them as a source for your advancement.

If you have a job, your colleagues and bosses are your audience and are there to watch how you execute your work. This is why some organizations have performance reviews. Do you have children or people who look up to you? They are your audience; their presence will question the integrity of your actions and will challenge you to be cautious of your lifestyle. As a teacher, your classroom is your stage; teaching is your performance, and the students are your audience. Their feedback will give you a hint on how to move to your next level.

Your spotlight

Every spotlight comes with an outstanding performance and is attainable when you stage a remarkable act for your audience. The acts must come from a place of consistency, determination, and continuity. Work smart, and work hard, be creative, and innovative in any task you are engaged in. Refuse to risk the best years of your spotlight to playing small.

Outstanding performance is like a voice, and it has the ability to speak. It announces you to the world, depending on how good you are. My purpose for writing this chapter is to let you know that ruling your world does not happen by accident. Give room for all your outstanding performances to pave the way to your spotlight.

The hidden performance

I was repeatedly advised to work from behind-the-scenes right from the inception of the childcare centre. As a person of colour, I was told that my accent would betray me. I adhered and worked from behind-the-scenes for several months. It was like denying my true identity and capabilities. I allowed someone else to perform the supervisory role while I took the back seat.

However, I carried out most of the supervisory jobs and trained the acting supervisor and staff from the background. It was a tough place to operate from; having to pay someone for all the supervisory jobs I did without getting the recognition for it. This lifestyle hit me so hard that I finally summoned the courage to take over the role. Shortly after I did, the narrative changed. I worked ten times harder to stabilize the processes and systems. It was not easy, but I'm glad I found the strength and courage to step up and debunked the fear that held me bound for a long time.

I showed up boldly in a peculiar way and took over the mantle of leadership. Things began to fall in place as soon as I did that. It was obvious that even though I was more than enough, but I lived a lie for a long time. The centre is currently making waves; it has grown in leaps and bounds with a second location in a span of three years. I conquered the very things that I feared the most.

Avoid letting fear suffocate your confidence, self-worth, and voice. Be brave. Don't be afraid of missing the mark a few times in an attempt to showcase a quality performance. And even if you do, trace your steps back to the drawing board, make the necessary corrections, and then set out again once you have figured out your next line of action. You can touch the sky if you don't give up.

The performer and performance

In as much as the performer and the performance are two different terms, however, they are deeply connected and inseparable. There is no performance without a performer;

neither is there a performer without a performance. Great performances are usually traceable to great performers.

I recently watched a five-minute video clip of a motivational speaker whose name I did not remember at the time. But in the end, I was hooked by his inspirational message, and I reminisced on it for days. Based on the way he crafted his speech; I searched and found his name. Since then, I have watched several of his videos due to his exceptional presentation.

People often hold great performers in the deep part of their hearts. Their performances never die; it lives on even when they are no more. These people leave a lasting legacy to pass on to the next generation. Ruling your world is a matter of choice; you can only become what you permit yourself to be. You have the choice to pass through the world unnoticed and ignored or to turn your performances into an unforgettable experience.

CHAPTER 15

Your Voice & Your Story

> *The one thing you have that nobody else has is you. Your voice, your mind, your story, your vision. So write and draw, and build and play, and dance and live as only you can* —Neil Gaiman

All the contents I have poured out from Chapters One to Fourteen of this book are my blueprints and winning strategies to becoming a pathfinder. As I take you through this last chapter, I hope it will leave you with indelible evidence of being a pathfinder, too. I have engraved my voice in this book and imprinted my story in the pages believing that it will equip you with the courage to sail through any rising tides. I am still a work in progress, trying hard to turn my imperfections to perfections. I have chronicled both my trials and triumphs; and how I overcame tough times.

There are places my voice may or may never be heard or reached, and there are also places where my voice may or may not be loud enough to amplify my story. I have chosen this book as one of the mediums to convey my voice and stories for people to pick a lesson or two from it.

People convey lessons in different ways. One of these could be through songs, speeches, or storytelling. Sometimes, I break down emotionally over some songs. In like manner, I also get inspired to take action depending on how passionate a speaker spoke. Some emotional stories have a way of piercing my heart and soul, and when this happens, it often leaves me in an emotional state. The dynamic and unique nature of our voices should not be under-estimated. The sound, texture, emotion, tone, and messages are all magically entwined, and above all, it does wonders in people's hearts.

The voice that moves you to tears is the same voice that can fill your heart and soul with laughter and joy. It can lift and also pull down. There is power in it. We often take our voice for granted because we have not given it the attention it deserves.

Your asset

Your voice and story are the only things that stick with you when everything else is gone. People may spend a fortune to acquire assets, but your voice is one of God's most valuable assets and gifts to you. Often, we overlook its importance, and we are ignorant of when and how to use it, other than to express ourselves. As an asset, it needs to be cherished and used positively. It is a symbol of our authority and power.

Your voice is an essential piece of your existence and cannot be isolated from you. It registers your presence irrespective of the location. How do you feel when you hear the voice of a loved one or friend over a phone? You talk, laugh, share stories, and get lost in conversation as if you are next to each other.

Conversely, one would be frustrated when they struggle to hear audibly; what is being said during a call, especially when the discussion is critical. Imagine a world without voices! It would be a world full of chaos and confusion. Our voices could be expressed through painting, speaking, writing, singing, crying, silence, looking and even dancing.

Everyone does not have to speak to convey a message. I have seen people shed tears because of how a singer sang; that is the perfect way for the singer and listener to express themselves. Sometimes, we shed tears just by seeing others cry; that is the voice of tears speaking. A painting can convey a stronger message more than a thousand words. Some draw inspiration from the pages of a book; that is the writer's voice, which does wonders to the readers' minds. Some write more than they speak, and so for them, writing is the best medium to express their voice. Silence also speaks; sometimes, it can be the loudest of all the voices.

While growing up, just by looking at my father's eyes without him uttering a word, I could tell that my silly actions needed to be corrected. Those looks spoke louder than many words. Others might express hurt or anger through tears. I have seen people who got stuck while sharing an emotional story, and without saying a word moved the audience to tears.

Have you ever seen a pregnant woman who is about to put to birth? Most times, the only way for her to expresses the gravity of her pain is by crying. Those tears speak volume;

it goes a long way to give an insight into her painful state. However, once the baby is born, the mother forgets all about the pain and embraces the joy of motherhood. "It was said by Friedrich Nietzsche, "That which does not kill us makes us stronger."

The power of voice

Your voice is powerful enough to frame your world. It could be likened to a signature. When you sign a cheque for someone to withdraw money from your bank account, your presence is no longer needed. Your signature is as good as your stamp of authority. It sets the tone of command for payment to be initiated. I sometimes stumble on document that requires collective signatures for the purpose of decision making. Those signatures are powerful; they are as important as your voice and can establish justice.

Despite the number of voices, we hear daily from everywhere, it would be alarming not to be able to identify that of our loved ones. Research shows that from the tender age of two months, babies can single out and respond to their mother's voice. As we grow older; regardless of the voices we hear every day; we can pick and choose what and who we want to listen to in life.

In the face of adversity, some voices empower us to confront our fears. As a Christian, the written word of God stands out for me in times of trouble. Those words are dependable, and I rely on them. Next is my parent's; it guides and keeps me on track, even as an adult. Apart from those voices, my husband's voice also plays a vital role in my decision making. Mine plays a critical role in the upbringing of my children. Some people also connect to my voice for their growth, like my mentees and those who look up to me. There will always be people who are attracted to your voice if you let loose of your story through it.

Own your voice — Speak up

I was afraid of speaking up for a long time for fear of not being heard. I depended on people to help me out in nearly everything. But a time came when I had to rise and speak for myself. There are moments when it is ideal for people to speak on your behalf, and a time comes when you have to take the responsibility of owning your voice. There is no better time than now.

When I was nine years old, I would send my younger brother to my parent to request something on my behalf because I was too afraid of being told "No." Back then, I believed his voice was more favourable and powerful than mine and could easily yield results. It often worked to my advantage and sometimes not. On several occasions, he would return to be reminded of my initial request because he had forgotten a chunk of the message before getting to my parent. Those with younger siblings might have a clue of this gimmick.

Have you been in a similar situation, where you asked someone to do the things you could do on your behalf? You relegated your power due to fear of rejection or lack of confidence. When this happens, it is like leaving your stage for someone else to run your show. The likelihood for them to omit some part of your message is high. Step up and own your voice; there is always a starting point to anything in life;

you must not be perfect for your voice to be heard. Making mistakes is part of the deal in the process of speaking up.

Your voice and your story go side by side; they are a great pair. When you have a story, find a voice, and when you have a voice, find a story. Your story and your voice are not yours to keep; inspire others with it and point them in the right path. You can keep your experience but not your story. By all means, make it a gift to people for their rising. If you cannot share your story with your voice, express yourself in a book, sing a song, dance, or paint.

Telling people how you walked the path is more authentic than someone else telling others how you walked your path. Take ownership of what is yours and shine. Leaving your story in the hands of others is like borrowing someone's voice to sing your song. Hoarding your experience only prolongs your spotlight and moment of shinning. Be bold enough to use any medium you are conversant with to share your story of trials to triumphs to impact your world.

Lend your voice to the voiceless. Let it be foot for the lame, hope to the hopeless, strength to the weak, and sight to the blind. Your voice can bring healing to a dying world. Some of us are great achievers because someone lent theirs to us. You can cause a change with yours, one day at a time and with one person at a time.

Stories that inspire

Even though we are different in our unique ways, however, our end goals are similar, which is to be successful in all we do. Everyone craves for success, and I am yet to find a person who is not. I am still searching for that one person who will be bold enough to declare, "I want to be a failure." Despite our battles in life, ultimately, we want to come out victorious in the end. Some of us have been through uncountable cycles of setbacks, but through it all, we were not consumed; we came out much better, and we are still standing tall and strong. You can choose to chronicle how you overcame hard times in a book to inspire and encourage others to hold on.

Stories of betrayals, repeated failures, school dropouts, business slow down, job loss, bereavement, childlessness, divorce, bankruptcy should not deter you. These are all captivating stories that can add colour and a touch of class to those with similar experiences. These people may be eager to learn about how you survived those battles. A shared experience is a problem half solved. Your story is a seed to your harvest. The severity of some issues can make people willing to pay to hear you tell your story from your heart and soul. It is an honour to be able to guide someone through hard times.

Those who have walked through tough seasons, gain experience in the process, which makes them relatable and authentic to those in the same predicament. It moves them to sympathize and empathize. If you have the experience, the world is looking for you because you are a valuable asset. People are waiting to listen to your story of hope. Most broken people often end up with the most amazing stories which usually ushers them to the pinnacle of their accomplishments.

Don't hold back the stories behind your survival. Those winning strategies can make you a sought-after and can change the narrative of your life for good. You can build a thriving path in business and career with your experiences and stories. Cherish your seasons of difficulties; they are an integral part of your success.

I decided to step forward to do my bit of story sharing with my own unique voice to help people become pathfinders. As soon as I took the bold step, people supported me in the process. I discovered that my world has been waiting for my manifestation long before I was ready to serve them. Whenever you are ready to share your story, remember that there will always be people waiting for your manifestation and to catch you before you fall. Refuse to wait for too long because time progresses.

Simplify your story

Simplified stories have a genuine way of attracting attention and penetrating hearts. Keep your stories real and easy to understand. True stories are born out of real-life experiences and can make you a masterpiece. Even though some experiences are complicated, try as much as possible to keep it simple. Complex stories don't sell; it wearies people. A life of impact is traceable to how well you craft and tell your story. When it is simple enough, it brings about clarity and is soothing to the listeners.

Sharing my stories with simplicity has been extremely rewarding and uplifting. I lived a lie for too long, believing and afraid that my failures and setback will stand against me. The stories I thought would be used as a weapon against my soaring; became instrumental to my greatness. Because of that, I have become a better and stronger person. I hope you will find the bravery to share yours too. Let's pass the baton of story sharing. Let's keep the flow alive! And make it happen in our lifetime. Yes! We can do it.

At last!

As the character, Ray said in the movie Uptown Girls: "Every story has an end. But in life, every ending is just a new beginning."

Everyone has a unique voice and story that needs to be heard. It is not ideal to compare your beginning to someone else's ending or your ending to someone else's beginning. I may not have attained the highest heights or climbed the highest mountains; however, I am not where I used to be. I chose to take the lead with my story, knowing that I have hit the finished line of being referred to as "An author." What only began as a dream has finally become a reality. In other words, dreams do come true.

You only have one voice and one life, and you can only live once and die once. Use your voice to share your authentic and unique stories. You never know where it will lead you to and whose life it will add a touch of class. Aspire to leave a blueprint that will help others become pathfinders. Life is short. Strive to empty yourself, and above all, engrave your name in the sands of time. Leave a legacy.

What do you want people to remember you for, at last? At the end of my sojourn here on earth, I want to look back and say, "Yes! I made a vow to give my all. I am at peace with myself because I gave those around me and the world the very best of me. I can now take a bow." I have long concluded that "Better is the end of a thing than the beginning." — Ecclesiastes 7:8. I am glad you held tight to this book to the end. I believe the end of this book will be the beginning of your success story. The world is waiting for you. Be Your Pathfinder.

Other Book from the Author

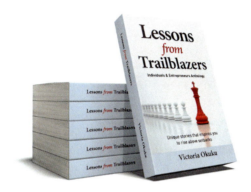

Lessons from Trailblazers

There is no self-sufficient human irrespective of their attainments in life. We learn every day, and everybody has the ability to change their lives for good. I am an embodiment of many things; author, educational consultant, mentor, business, and transformational strategist because I availed myself to learn from people who have gone ahead of me. This book houses unique stories from twenty-three different individuals who have successfully turned their trials to triumphs despite the odds that stood against them. Learning, some say, is a lifelong affair. The stories in this book will inspire you to sail above the waves during tough times.